USDA

United States
Department
of Agriculture

Forest Service

Rocky Mountain
Research Station

Research Paper
RMRS-RP-96

September 2012

Predicting Fire Severity Using Surface Fuels and Moisture

Pamela G. Sikkink
Robert E. Keane

ABSTRACT

Fire severity classifications have been used extensively in fire management over the last 30 years to describe specific environmental or ecological impacts of fire on fuels, vegetation, wildlife, and soils in recently burned areas. New fire severity classifications need to be more objective, predictive, and ultimately more useful to fire management and planning. Our objectives were to (1) quantify the relationships between fuel loading and moisture characteristics of surface fuels and the temperature and energy produced during combustion, and (2) to produce a classification that summarized these relationships into unique, realistic classes of fire severity. Using computer simulation, we created 115,280 synthetic fuel beds with diverse compositions and moisture conditions and burned them using computer simulation with the First Order Fire Effects Model (FOFEM). Using average fire intensity, fire residence time, total fuel consumed, depth of soil heating, and temperature in the top 1 cm of soil, we created a nine-group classification that separated fire severity classes based first on soil heating, second on intensity and fire time, and third on fuel consumed. Fuel beds were correctly placed into the nine fire severity classes 98% of the time using subsets of the synthetic fuel beds.

Keywords: Computer simulation, fire effects, FOFEM, fuelbed, hierarchical clustering

ACKNOWLEDGMENTS

This project was funded by the Joint Fire Sciences Program project #09-1-07-4. We thank Larry Gangi, Systems for Environmental Management, for customizing outputs of FOFEM and troubleshooting outputs from the synthetic dataset runs. Kevin Ryan, Dan Jimenez, Jim Reardon, Duncan Lutes, L. Scott Baggett, and Elizabeth Reinhardt, all of the U.S. Forest Service Rocky Mountain Research Station, provided technical assistance, advice on running FOFEM, and many other discussions throughout the duration of the study. We thank the fire managers and technicians who provided input and suggestions on the moisture scenarios, including Dave Brownlie, Allen Carter, and Rick Vollick, U.S. Fish and Wildlife Service; Tom Remus, Bureau of Indian Affairs; Cody Wienk, National Park Service; and Eugene Watkins and Zack Riggs, U.S. Forest Service. Art Sikkink provided assistance with the Visual Basic macro; and L. Scott Baggett, RMRS, programmed the cluster analysis procedure in SAS. Benjamin Bird, RMRS, created the figure showing class membership within the moisture scenarios. The cover photograph was taken by Michael Harrington, RMRS Missoula Fire Sciences Laboratory, and is used with permission. We thank reviewers Kevin Ryan and Theresa Jain, RMRS, and Penelope Morgan, University of Idaho, whose comments and suggestions greatly improved this manuscript.

CONTENTS

Predicting Fire Severity Using Surface Fuels and Moisture

Pamela G. Sikkink and Robert E. Keane

Introduction

Fire severity classifications have been used extensively in fire management over the last 30 years to address specific environmental or ecological impacts of fire on fuels, vegetation, wildlife, and soils in recently burned areas (Azuma et al. 2004; Boby et al. 2010; Carey et al. 2003; Jain et al. 2012). For example, managers and researchers have used fire severity classifications to evaluate prescribed fire success (Ryan and Noste 1985), stratify post-fire vegetation and soil response (Parsons et al. 2010), and describe burn patterns (Carey et al. 2003). Severity classifications have also been used to assess rehabilitation potential (Kuenzi et al. 2008; Robichaud et al. 2003) and decide whether burn impacts can be mitigated on a landscape (Beschta et al. 2004; Robichaud et al. 2007a). They have been correlated with remotely sensed images to develop maps that delineate areas to target efforts to reduce erosion, plant seedlings, and restore native plants (Beschta et al. 2004; Miller et al. 2003; Parsons 2003). Patterns of fire or burn severity have also been used to delineate fire regimes (Heyerdahl et al. 2012; Morgan et al. 2001), link landscape patterns and scales of disturbance processes (Chuvieco 1999; Dillon et al. 2011; Hudak et al. 2007; Turner et al. 1994), assess post-fire vegetation recovery and reestablishment (Díaz-Delgado et al. 2003; Lentile et al. 2007; Turner et al. 1999), and evaluate disturbance of wildlife habitat (Zarriello et al. 1995) and the effects of fire on species of concern (Kotliar et al. 2003). All of these fire and burn severity classifications are post-fire assessments that have some relationship to the response of interest, but little predictive power because they are (1) limited in scope; (2) inconsistent; (3) not directly tied to fire characteristics and/or (4) lack a distinct quantitative basis for each class.

The main problems with most current fire severity classifications are that they are tailored to meet the needs of a specific application and the data used to create them have been reduced to highly subjective, simplistic classes. Specialized classifications collapse complex interactions between fire, fuels, biota, and the biophysical environment into an over-simplified and over-generalized three- to six-group ordinal scale classification. Most of the classifications are ultimately reduced to classes of "low," "moderate," or "high" that represent a synthesis of the complex and interacting effects of a fire (Ryan and Noste 1985). The advantage of these simple indices is that they integrate a variety of information and summarize it into succinct, intuitive categories useful to management. The disadvantage is that they are overly simplistic and rarely address all possible management concerns that require an estimate of severity (Lutes et al. 2006). Subjective, simplistic classifications are difficult to teach. They are also difficult to use consistently in the field because individuals assess severity using qualitative or semi-quantitative evaluation criteria differently based on their previous experiences evaluating fire and fuels. Ultimately, most of these fire severity classifications have little predictive power to describe potential fire severity before a site actually burns because an explicit cause-and-effect relationship has not been developed between the fuels and the fires that consume them.

A fire severity classification should directly relate the interaction of fire, fuels, biota, and the biophysical environment. Ideally, empirical data should include a wide variety of fuel beds and moisture scenarios that, when burned, lead to values for heat production, burn time, consumption, and other fire effects that form an objective fire-severity continuum. Through robust statistical analysis, the continuum is partitioned into distinct classes based on fuel bed and moisture parameters. As new technologies become available and are adopted (e.g., high resolution remote sensing products, mechanistic simulation modeling, and innovative sampling techniques), burn severity classifications will increasingly need to describe complex fire effects based on physical characteristics of a fire and quantitative assessment variables, much like those used by fire behavior and many other fields of ecology.

This study was conducted to (1) demonstrate a technique for developing future fire severity classifications that are compatible with developing technologies in fuels research and (2) to produce a classification comprised of unique, realistic classes that objectively relate fire and fuel characteristics to their associated fire effects. To meet these objectives, we used computer-simulated burning of real and synthetic fuel beds and examined the quantitative relationships between fuel characteristics, moisture, fire intensity, and first-order fire effects. Our results were somewhat constrained by the underlying assumptions of our simulation model, but using simulation burning was the only practical method to effectively treat the full range of fuels and moistures required to build an effective classification. We defined our fire severity classes by the degree of changes in the direct first-order fire effects, including the amount of fuels consumed, degree of change in vegetation and soil biota due to soil heating, and smoke production. Although the proposed classification is based solely on surface fuels, it can be used in fire planning or fuel treatments efforts with some simple precautions. We also suggest several ways to refine and improve this classification for fire managers.

Background

The terms burn severity, fire severity, and fire intensity have been confused among scientists and managers for many years (Jain 2004; Lentile et al. 2006). Burn severity and fire severity are often used interchangeably to describe the degree of above- and below-ground organic matter consumption during a fire (Jain 2004; Keeley 2009; National Wildfire Coordinating Group 2006). Fire or burn severity are also used as general terms for the degree of environmental change caused by fires or as a specific loss of organic matter or biomass above and below ground that is caused by the burning process (Keeley 2009; National Wildfire Coordinating Group 2006). In contrast, the term *fire intensity* is used for units of heat and describes the physical combustion process (Byram and Nelson 1952; Rothermel 1972). This report uses the terms *fire intensity* in its traditional sense. We reserve *burn severity* to denote classifications created for remote sensing applications because the term has a long history of use in the remote-sensing field (Dillon et al. 2011; Lentile et al. 2006; Lentile et al. 2007). We use *fire severity* to denote the magnitude of fire-caused damage to vegetation and fuels and general descriptions of fire impacts, such as fire effects on soil (Simard 1991). We use the term *surface fuels* to encompass all fuels that lay above the mineral soil A horizon. Technically, duff would be a *ground fuel* (Anderson 1982; O'Brien 2004), which burns differently during the fire combustion process than litter and larger fuels; but for simplicity in writing, we chose to refer to all fuels in this study as surface fuels.

Many fire and burn severity classification systems have been developed to describe specific fire effects using general categories of fire damage. However, these classifications are limited to qualitative descriptions of specific environmental effects associated with burning. For example, fire severity classifications have been created to describe fire-caused damage to coniferous forests (Bradley et al. 1992; Schimmel and Granstrom 1996), aspen (Brown and DeByle 1987), and taiga (Foote 1983). Ryan and Noste (1985) created a general classification for fire effects focused on fire intensity and duration that was expanded to include spatial and temporal effects in boreal forests (Ryan 2002). Some describe fire effects specifically on tree crowns (Jain and Graham 2007); others specifically classify fire effects on soil (Huffman et al. 2001; Hungerford 1996; Jain et al. 2006; Lewis et al. 2006; Parsons 2003; Parsons et al. 2010; Tarrant 1956; Wells et al. 1979). Other severity classifications have been created for fire effects in vegetation and vegetation recovery after wildfire (Moreno and Oechel 1989; USDA 2010). Perhaps the most commonly used fire severity classification is the Composite Burn Index (CBI) that quantifies severity from soil color, vegetation reduction, and fuel consumption (Key 2005; Key and Benson 1999).

Normalized Burn Ratio (NBR), and the related differenced NBR (dNBR) (Key and Benson 2006) and relativized dNBR (RdNBR) (Miller and Thode 2007), are commonly used to infer burn severity from remotely sensed images (Singh 1989). Often differences in reflectivity between pre-burn and post-burn landscapes are classified for severity based on how great those differences are and this has been related to specific vegetation responses (Brumby et al. 2001; Epting et al. 2005; Redmond and Winne 2001; Wang and Glenn 2009; White et al. 1996).

The sensitivity of CBI and NBR to severity measures have been assessed by Key (2006), Kasischke et al. (2008), Murphy et al. (2008), and De Santis and Chuvieco (2007), among others. CBI and NBR have been adjusted for new burn severity indices that include leaf area index (Boer et al. 2008), relativization of the NBR (Miller and Thode 2007), and the use of additional imagery including pre- and post-fire images (Norton et al. 2009; Robichaud et al. 2007b; van Wagendonk et al. 2004). While each of these tools are useful for obtaining a relative assessment of fire effects on a specific environmental feature or landscape, each is also limited in application because a physical measure of fire behavior (e.g., fire intensity) is not objectively related to a quantified fire effect caused by combustion of a specific fuel load.

In contrast to fire and burn severity classifications based on subjective, categorical, post-burn assessments described in the examples above, three severity classifications have been created using quantitative measures. Two were developed in British Columbia using duff plus slash consumption and/or depth of burn to assign fire severity (Feller 1998; Trowbridge et al. 1989). The third classification was developed in Spain; it used experimental burns to quantify soil temperatures and loss of biomass during burning of shrub ecosystems (Perez and Moreno 1998). Although all of these classifications have a quantitative component to their development, none are based on the full range of fuels that would commonly be found in forest, shrub, and grassland ecosystems. None relate the fire intensity achieved during a burn directly to resulting fire effects, and none can be used to predict fire severity before a fire occurs.

Burning the hundreds of thousands of different fuel bed compositions needed to create an adequate classification that can predict burn severity is expensive and time consuming, and a major reason why few comprehensive fire severity classifications based on fuels exist. Linking the heat produced by a fuel bed with its fire effects requires instrumentation and manpower to gather pre-burn, concurrent, and post-burn information on fuel biomass and moisture values, fire heat and residence time, and fire effects. Capturing the range of fire severity possible from the variation within fuels and fire effects requires many such instrumented burns. Before an objective fire severity classification could be developed, alternatives to actual burning had to be developed that could "burn" fuel beds using controlled inputs and conditions and that could output relevant characteristics of the fire and resulting fire effects. Fire models (i.e., algorithms that represent different burn conditions) have greatly improved our ability to understand the burning process (Albini and Reinhardt 1995; Linn et al. 2005; Rothermel 1972). Computer programs that model fuel combustion and fire effects, which are based on Albini's (1976; 1994) pioneering work on the relationship between fire intensity and fuels, created the means for linking fire intensity, fuel characteristics, and fire effects. Because they are computer models, they can also be manipulated to output the specific variables required to evaluate the range of fuel bed compositions that are needed to create a comprehensive fire severity classification.

Methods

Fire Simulation

The First Order Fire Effects Model (FOFEM) was used to simulate fire behavior and effects for our two datasets (Keane et al. 2008; Reinhardt et al. 1997). FOFEM was selected over other models that predict fire effects because it (1) calculates soil heating to 13 cm (5 in) deep, (2) is limited to surface burns (i.e., does not simulate crown fires), and (3) uses a batch input file to simulate combustion in a large number of fuel beds at one time. In addition, we worked with the FOFEM programmers to modify the tool and output several customized variables, including four measures of fire intensity (mean intensity, median intensity, sum of intensity during a burn, and maximum intensity reached during a burn), the temperatures and durations of heating in each 1-cm thick soil layer, and the depth of the deepest soil layer reaching 60 °C and 275 °C (see Keane et al. 2008, http://frames.nbii.gov/portal/server.pt/community/fofem/613).

Several assumptions were made for the simulation burns. Some were inherent to the FOFEM simulation program; others were made during data preparation. FOFEM assumes that all fuels within a fuel bed will burn; that is, there is no patchiness or variability to the burn (Reinhardt et al. 1997). FOFEM has no spatial or landscape component to its burns as would be inherent in wildfire or prescribed burns. FOFEM also allocates proportions of each fuel component to flaming and smoldering combustion depending on a moisture description assigned by the user; we assumed that our moisture conditions, which were assigned "wet" to "very dry" based on moisture scenario, were within the ranges assigned in FOFEM and were handled appropriately for each combustion type. As modelers, we assumed that FOFEM would pick the most appropriate algorithms for burning the fuels and that each fuel bed we created would burn (i.e., no fuel beds or moisture scenarios would be outside the range of FOFEM's predictive algorithms). We assumed that FOFEM contained predictive algorithms that could realistically burn fuel beds for the full range of duff in our study although evidence has been found to the contrary (Hood et al. 2007). We know that the ranges of duff thickness and biomass are biased in FOFEM algorithms toward fuels of the interior west (Brown et al. 1985) and that many of our duff measures extend beyond these ranges. This probably affected some class characteristics, but we do not know to what degree. Finally, we assumed that assigning the same moisture distribution for all fuel beds, and assigning rot percent to the 1000-hr fuels using only five categories instead of a continuum, would not adversely affect the burning or classification process.

FOFEM requires specific inputs on several climatic, soil, and moisture distribution factors that were not an integral part of the datasets created or compiled for this study so we assigned the default values from FOFEM to these factors. In addition to the actual and synthetic fuel loadings and moistures by component, we added values within the program for burning season (summer), duff moisture distribution (even), region (interior west), soil type (coarse-silt), and fuel type (natural). FOFEM was run in batch mode and fires were simulated for 8,000 seconds to calculate the median. Settings for the FOFEM runs included a limit of 10% fire intensity under zero duff conditions and use of the original burn up time if duff was present.

Datasets

Two datasets were used to create and verify this fire severity classification for surface fuels. One dataset, the "synthetic dataset," was computer generated and used exclusively to develop the classification; the simulated fuel beds that were generated for it are referred to as the "synthetic fuel beds." The second dataset consisted of actual field data, which provided realistic limits on fuel loads for each of the synthetic fuel components and served as an independent dataset to verify the uniqueness of the classes created in the classification process. This dataset is referred to as the "actual dataset" and its fuel beds are called "actual fuel beds." The fuel components comprising both the synthetic and actual fuel beds include the following commonly accepted U.S. size classes (Fosberg 1970):

- Duff
- Litter
- Fine woody debris (FWD)
  - 1-hr fuels: particles with diameters <0.64 cm (<0.25 in) in diameter (1 hr refers to the number of hours it takes debris of this size to dry enough to reach equilibrium moisture content.)
  - 10-hr fuels: particles between 0.64 and 2.54 cm (0.25-1.00 in) in diameter
  - 100-hr fuels: particles 2.54 to 7.62 cm (1-3 in) in diameter
- Coarse woody debris (CWD)
  - 1000-hr fuels consisted of fuel components >7.62 cm (>3 inches) in diameter. This class included all logs. Rot categories were assigned to CWD during the fuel-bed creation process.
- Live shrubs
- Herbs

The following paragraphs describe the development of the synthetic and actual datasets, including a description of the variables added to each dataset to do the simulation burning.

Synthetic Dataset

The synthetic dataset was created by randomly assigning fuel loadings to each fuel component and systematically combining the eight fuel components into a synthetic fuel bed. All loadings and assignments were made using Visual Basic for Applications in Microsoft Access ©. Loading values were randomly assigned to

Table 1—Ranges of increasing biomass (kg m^{-2}) and percent rot used to systematically create the fuel components of each synthetic fuel bed.

We created 11,528 simulated fuel beds using nested loop routines within Visual Basic for Applications (VBA). We defined upper and lower limits for each of the four major fuel components and percent rot according to study objectives; then we created intervals within those limits from which we generated random numbers for the biomass of each fuel component. Components were nested in order of: (1) litter biomass, 6 intervals; (2) coarse woody debris biomass, 9 intervals; (3) percent rot of coarse woody debris, 5 intervals; (4) duff biomass, 11 intervals; and (5) fine woody debris biomass, 4 intervals. Herb and shrubs were randomly assigned biomass values for each fuel bed from within their respective interval. Fine woody debris was further subdivided into biomass values for 1-hr, 10-hr, and 100-hr fuels. To fit the input parameters of FOFEM, duff biomass was converted to duff depth using a duff density value. Several checks were made after the fuel components were combined into a fuel bed to eliminate combinations of fuels or characteristics that could not exist; for example, no rot percentage was assigned if there was no coarse woody debris.

Biomass intervals for each surface fuel component (kg m^{-2})

Increment	Duff	Litter	Total fine woody debris	Coarse woody debris	Herb	Shrub	Coarse woody decay/rot (%)
1	0.00-0.01	0-0.20	0-0.53	0-1.01	0-2.02	0-8.97	0.00
2	0.01-0.42	0.21-0.57	0.54-6.74	1.02-1.83			20.00
3	0.43-1.11	0.58-2.41	6.75-22.42	1.84-2.25			40.00
4	1.12-2.97	2.42-11.22	22.43-44.84	2.26-3.56			60.00
5	2.98-4.23	11.23-33.64		3.57-6.34			80.00
6	4.24-4.86	33.65-67.25		6.35-7.86			
7	4.87-5.89			7.87-22.42			
8	5.90-8.44			22.43-44.84			
9	8.45-13.40			44.85-89.67			
10	13.41-22.42						
11	22.43-78.47						
12	78.48-156.92						

each fuel component from their respective loading ranges as described in Table 1. Coarse woody debris (CWD) values were assigned a random percent rot value within the systematic process to satisfy FOFEM input requirements (Reinhardt et al. 1997) and simulate more realistic field conditions for CWD. Foliage or branches from tree sources were not included in the loading assignment process because they were not considered surface fuels. The values in Table 1 were initially derived for the fuel loading models (FLMs) developed by Lutes (2009) and they are currently used to map national fuel layers (U.S. Department of the Interior 2011). FLMs were developed from actual field data so they were ecologically based and resulted in realistic ranges for the fuel components. Because the fuel bed data used to create the FLMs came from a limited number of sample areas across the United States, however, we increased the range of FLM fuel loadings for our study by adding two to three additional ranges to each fuel component at the top end of each FLM range. This expanded our range of variability and at least doubled maximum loadings in the actual data set to include fuel beds that may not have yet been sampled. We did not evaluate whether all of the synthetic fuel beds that were created for this study actually existed in nature.

Distributing the fuels systematically into beds resulted in 11,528 individual fuel beds that contained fuel loading values for eight fuel components, a range of duff depths, and a variety of rot values for the CWD component. The fuel loads ranged from minimal to heavy loadings and the systematic assignment of variable values allowed us to limit the total number of fuel beds for analysis. We initially experimented with systematically increasing biomass for each component using a set loading for each fuel type instead of assigning random loadings within intervals for each; however, many fuel beds with low biomass were duplicated and

USDA Forest Service RMRS-RP-96. 2012.

so many fuel beds were generated that computational times for statistical analysis and graphing were impractical. Alternately, assigning loadings or biomass by true random methods did not guarantee a wide range of fuel bed compositions as did the assignment of loadings within intervals. Assigning fuel loads by systematic increases within defined intervals was ultimately the most practical method to insure a wide range of fuel loadings and a reasonable number of fuel beds for analysis and classification. The same rationale was used to limit the ranges of the synthetic fuel components to double those of the actual fuel beds. If we used a wider range of values for each component, more fuel beds would be created using the systematic process.

The two exceptions to assigning loadings using the FLM intervals were in the assignments of the fine-woody debris and shrub/herb components. Fine woody debris (FWD) was not separated into individual components (i.e., 1-, 10-, and 100-hr fuels) within the FLMs, but the individual components were required by FOFEM for the simulation burn. To make these assignments, we randomly picked a total for FWD from the appropriate FWD intervals in Table 1; we then divided that number by two and selected random values for 1-hr and 10-hr components within this new limit. New 1-hr and 10-hr components were then subtracted from the total FWD with the remainder assigned to the 100-hr loading. We assigned shrub and herb loadings to each fuel bed using random values over a single range that was twice the loading values for these components that occurred in the actual data set (described in the next section).

Moisture values for the duff, 10-hr, 1000-hr, and soil were assigned to each of the 11,528 fuel beds using 10 different moisture scenarios (Table 2). The moisture scenarios were designed by managers from the western and northeastern United States, the Midwest, and Florida; they emulated different conditions that are used to guide wildfire and prescription-burn decisions around the country. By using scenarios with vastly different moisture criteria, we ensured that a range of fire effects were simulated. Ultimately, we generated 115,280 synthetic fuel beds (11,528 fuel beds x 10 moisture scenarios) for the classification process.

Actual Dataset

The actual data set was comprised of 4,046 fuel beds sampled from field sites throughout the contiguous United States. The field sites were all sampled using established sampling protocols. The data set was compiled by Lutes et al. (2009),

Table 2—Moisture values (%) assigned to the synthetic and actual datasets before simulation burning with the First Order Fire Effects Model (FOFEM).

Scenarios were constructed for regions or areas based on input from fire managers in the western United States (West), northeastern United States (NE), Florida and West Virginia (FL), and South Dakota (SD) for prescribed burns (Prescribed) and wildfires (see Applicable areas column). Scenario G includes the settings used to create the original fue loading models (FLMs) of Lutes et al. (2009). All moisture scenarios should be applicable across the United States and internationally.

Scenario	10-H moisture	1000-H moisture	Duff moisture	Soil moisture	Condition	Examples of applicable areas
A	4	10	20	5	Very dry fuels, duff, and soil	Wildfire West & NE
B	4	20	125	5	Dry fuels and soil with wet duff	Prescribed West
C	6	15	50	10	Dry fuels with moderate duff moisture	West, very dry in FL
D	8	20	100	15	Moderately dry fuels with wet duff	Dry FL, prescribed NE
E	8	75	75	20	Moderately dry fuels and duff, wet soil	Prescribed West, FL, & NE
F	8	25	175	25	Dry fuels, wet duff and wet soil	Prescribed FL & NE
G	10	15	40	10	Dry fuels , moderate duff moisture	FLM burn scenario
H	10	20	100	15	Moderately wet fuel and soil, wet duff	West, FL, NE; prescribed NE,FL
I	10	20	175	25	Wet fuels, duff, and soil	Prescribed FL
J	12	40	35	20	Wet fuels and soil, dry duff	Averages for prescribed in SD

who used the fuel beds to create a fuels classification that would predict smoke particulate and soil heating when surface fuels burned. Fuel beds from the Fuel Characteristic Classification System (Ottmar et al. 2007; Prichard et al. 2006) were also embedded within the FLM analyses (Lutes et al. 2009). Each fuel bed consisted of biomass values for litter, duff, 1-hr, 10-hr, 100-hr, and 1000-hr fuels; but a constant value was assigned to herb and shrub components. Like the synthetic dataset, fire behavior and effects were simulated for each of the fuel beds under the 10 moisture scenarios, resulting in a data set with 40,460 total fuel beds. For this study, the actual dataset fulfilled two functions: (1) it provided field values for the loads of each fuel component and (2) it served as an independent dataset to verify the severity classes developed with the synthetic dataset and validate the classification.

Data Analyses

Before classification analysis, we verified that we met two important objectives for the synthetic fuel beds, which were to (1) double the range of load values in the actual data set, and (2) create combinations of fuels that did not exist within the actual data set. Box plots were used to evaluate the ranges of each fuel type in the actual and synthetic data sets. The range of compositions and fuel ratios within the actual and synthetic fuel beds (objective 2) were tested using a piper diagram within Sigma Plot (Systat Software Inc. 2008).

Twenty-eight independent variables were available for statistical and classification analysis from the FOFEM outputs including 14 fire effects (fuel consumption and soil heating) and 14 fire behavior variables (Table 3). These outputs were stored in each of the two datasets using a fuel-bed identification number. The identification number contained a code letter for moisture scenario and a number relating

Table 3—Outputs for each fuel bed after simulation burning using First Order Fire Effects Model (FOFEM). Variables used in cluster analysis are shown in bold.

Type	Output	Units	Abbreviation for output
Fire effect	Fuel consumption for nine fuel components (e.g., Duff consumed = DuffC)	kg m^{-2}	DuffC, LitC, DW1C, DW10C, DW100C, HerC, ShrC.
	Fuel consumption for downed woody 1000-hr fuels (DW1k), solid (Snd) and rotten(Rot)	kg m^{-2}	DW1kSndC, DW1kRotC
	Fuel consumption for crown canopy foliage and branches (not used in this study)	kg m^{-2}	FolC, BraC
	Total biomass of all fuels consumed during combustion	kg m^{-2}	**TotCon**
	Maximum temperature reached for various soil depths	°C	S0 (temperate at surface), **S1**...... to S13 (temperature at 1 to 13 cm below surface)
	Maximum depth to reach 60°C or 275°C	cm	**SL60**, SL275
	Mineral soil exposure after burn	%	MSEPer
	Reduction in duff depth	cm	DDRed
Physical properties of fire during burn	Fire intensity measures (mean, median, maximum, and sum)	Kw/m^2	**FIAvg**, FIMed, FIMax, FISum
	Fire intensity attributed to vegetation (S=shrub; H=herb; F=foliage; B=branch)	Kw/m^2	FISHFB
	Duration of fire	sec	**FTime**
	Duration of flames	sec	FlaDur
	Duration of smoke	sec	SmoDur

to the fuel bed (e.g., E11575 was fuel bed 11575 burned using moisture scenario E). All original fuel-bed compositions, moisture values, and FOFEM outputs were stored in the relational database to export the different combinations of variables selected for statistical analysis or classification procedures.

Several assumptions were made related to the classification process that affected the final product, but they were assumptions that we felt were normal to make. We assumed that creating widely diverse fuel beds would produce the greatest range of fire behavior and effects and represent the entire set of fuel beds in the United States. We assumed that current burning models (specifically FOFEM) were rigorous and progressive enough to provide relative, unbiased predictions; and we assumed that clustering the variability in fire characteristics generated from diverse fuel beds into a small number of classes would reduce redundancy across classes and provide an objective way to describe fire effects.

A variety of data exploration techniques were used to decide which FOFEM output variables would be most useful to create groups from the synthetic and actual data sets. Descriptive statistics were run within SAS (SAS Institute Inc. 2008) on each of the moisture scenarios to explore means and standard deviations for output variables. Histograms and box plots were constructed to explore the fuel-bed distributions. QQ tests were performed on individual variables to test for normal distribution of the data and subjected to common transformations when found to be non-normally distributed. If data were not normally distributed, non-parametric statistics were used to test differences in variables between moisture scenarios and between cluster groups. Correlation coefficients were computed in SAS using the Spearman's rank and Pearson's correlations on the input variables for the various run scenarios and the output variables from FOFEM used in cluster analysis. Cutoff values for correlations using these two tests were 0.80 with those variables exceeding the cutoff eliminated from further analysis. Eliminated variables included flame duration and several measures of fire intensity among others. Kruskal-Wallis non-parametric one-way ANOVA tests were run in SAS to determine if each variable differed in means between moisture scenarios. Those variables that had significant differences between scenarios were considered more likely to show significant differences when all the moisture scenarios were combined for the classification analysis. Differences were considered significant if $p<0.05$.

Creating Groups

Classification of the fuel beds was accomplished through agglomerative hierarchical cluster analysis using PROC CLUSTER and the Lance-Williams Flexible Beta method in the SAS statistical package (SAS Institute Inc. 2008). Eight FOFEM output variables were suitable to use for clustering each data set because they showed significant differences in FOFEM runs across all moisture scenarios: average fire intensity (FIAvg in kw m^{-2}), fire residence time (FTime, sec), total fuels consumed (TotCon, kg m^{-2}), smoke duration (SmoDur, sec), maximum temperature reached at one centimeter below the surface (S1, °C), deepest soil depth to reach 60 °C (SL60, cm), duff depth (DuffDep, cm), and 1000-hr moisture (CWDMoist, %). Values for each of these outputs were standardized within SAS and the standardized values were used in all statistical analyses and clustering procedures. Raw values corresponding to these standardized values were only used to illustrate points on the cluster dendrograms and tables to make the diagrams easier to understand.

Cluster analysis trials were run using three, four, and five of the eight potential variables in different combinations. Five variables (FIAvg, TotCon, FTime, S1, and SL60) were ultimately selected for hierarchical clustering because they (1) showed significant differences between moisture scenario runs using Kruskal-Wallis comparisons (p-value <0.05); (2) represented a range of factors, including time, intensity, depth of burn, and consumption; and (3) could be consistently estimated in some way by managers on site after a fire. Group characteristics were tested for six, seven, and nine groups before the final cluster procedure was run to completion. For each group, means and standard deviations of the five variables were summarized to determine what the differences were between groups. Cubic Clustering Criterion, Pseudo-F and Pseudo-t-squared tests were also used within SAS to help assess the optimal number of clusters. In this paper, we use the terms clusters, classes, and groups to refer to the groups created during this hierarchical clustering process.

Verifying Groups

We tested burn severity class compositions using three methods to determine whether the classes created by the clustering procedure with the synthetic data were distinct enough to group the same way using different data or grouping techniques. First, we analyzed the actual dataset using the same procedure used to cluster the synthetic data. Because clustering results are often different if data within a single data set are changed or removed (McCune and Grace 2002), we used an entirely new dataset as a strong test of whether the classes were unique and repeatable. Hierarchical cluster analysis of the actual data set was conducted with the same five variables and pruned to the same number of groups as the synthetic data set to determine if the same variables were controlling the clustering of each (i.e., similar variables were controlling branching in each branch of the cluster dendrogram). Next, the same five variables used in cluster analysis were analyzed using classification and regression tree analysis (CART) on both the synthetic and actual data sets. We compared the characteristics of classes created in the CART with the classes created in cluster analysis to see if the same variables were important to differentiating classes in both the synthetic and actual datasets. CART results provided an independent evaluation of the cohesiveness of each class's characteristics, as well as an alternative measure of classification error, because CART uses different procedures to create groups than hierarchical clustering (McCune and Grace 2002; Nisbet et al. 2009; Venables and Ripley 2002). Finally, we tested the repeatability of the classes with non-parametric discriminant analysis (DA) on the synthetic data set. Discriminant analysis compared clustered classes made using a subset of the synthetic data to the classification made using the entire synthetic dataset to give estimates of the percentages of misclassifications within each group (McCune and Grace 2002). We conducted discriminant analysis using the five standardized variables and cluster as the grouping variable. We used non-parametric discriminant analysis in the SAS set with kernel = normal, r =0.3, and pool = yes. The value for the smoothing parameter r was computed as a weighted group mean based on the number of fuel beds in each cluster and on using five variables for the analysis as instructed in SAS.

Results

Data Exploration

To create an objective fire severity classification that would be applicable to the wide variety of fuels and fuel-bed compositions found across the United States, we needed to create a dataset that expanded the known limits of fuel loadings and fuel-component combinations of previously sampled fuel-beds in the United States. Our goal was to double the range of each fuel component and examine the combustion effects over the expanded range. In the actual data set, the loads falling between the 25th to 75th percentiles on the box plot were less than 2.2 kg m^{-2} (10 T ac^{-1}) for all components. Maximum duff load was less than 90 kg m^{-2} (400 T ac^{-1}) (Fig. 1a). For our synthetic data set, the 25th to 75th percentiles fell between 3.4 to 15.5 kg m^{-2} (15 and 70 T ac^{-1}) (Fig. 1b). Maximum duff load was identical to the actual dataset but the value was considered unimportant because FOFEM treats extremely high duff loads identically during the simulation burns. All other fuel components met the objective of double the actual fuel biomass.

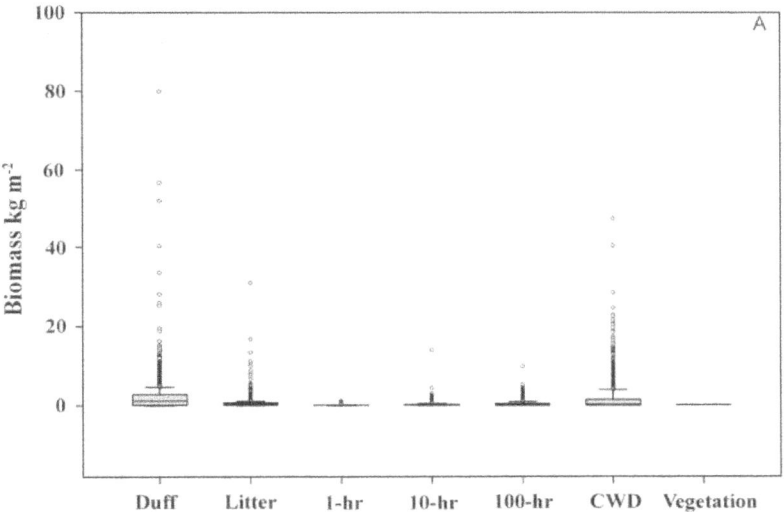

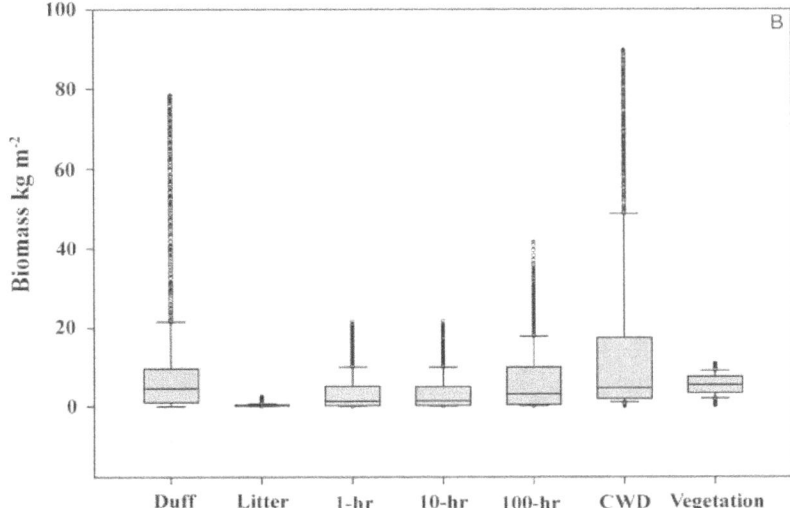

Figure 1—Range of biomass values in kg m^{-2} for each of the fuel types in (A) the actual data set, n = 4,046 (Lutes et al. 2009); and (B) the synthetic data set, n = 11,528. CWD = Coarse-woody debris (1000-hr) fuels. Vegetation = total for shrub and herb loadings combined. Conversion factor for biomass in tons acre^{-1} = kg m^{-2} * 4.4609.

In addition to expanding the load limits of each individual fuel component (Fig. 1), combining those components within the fuel beds into new proportions was also important to creating a fire severity classification that encompassed a wide variety of fuel beds, combustion characteristics, and fire effects. For example, a fuel bed consisting of 100% duff measured at 150 kg m² creates different fire intensities and fire effects during simulated combustion than a fuel bed with 150 kg m⁻² of fuel comprised of 65 km² duff, 10 kg m⁻² FWD, and 75 kg m⁻² CWD, for a ratio of 64%: 4%: 32% on the fuel bed, respectively. If our classification process lacked fuel beds with certain ratios of fuel components (e.g., there were no fuel beds with a 25%, 50%, and 25% duff-FWD-CWD combination), our fire severity classification would not adequately represent fire effects that would result from fuel beds having this combination. Filling in missing proportions of fuel components during our data creation phase was important to ensuring that the maximum possible combinations of fuel-bed compositions were included in our burn simulations. As a result of the data creation process, gaps in the ratios of fuel components in the actual data (Fig. 2a) appeared to be adequately covered in the synthetic data set (Fig. 2b). Many new proportions of fuel components were created to fill in the white (gap) areas of the actual dataset and only a small area exists in the high proportions of 10-hr and low proportions of 100-hr fuels that remain unfilled (Fig. 2, lower right corner).

A

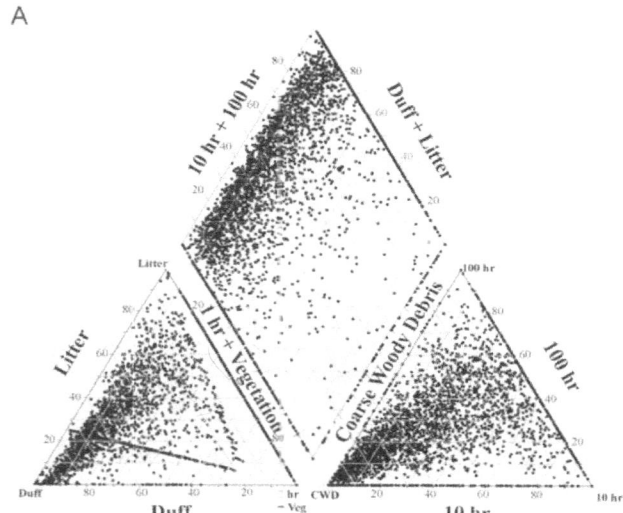

Figure 2—Piper diagram showing proportion of each fuel component within individual fuel beds. (A) actual data set (n = 4046); (B) synthetic data set (n = 11528). Each dot on the piper diagram shows the makeup of one fuel bed; its position determined by percentage of each fuel type that is found within the fuel bed. The lower left triangle consists of the smallest fuels; the lower right, the largest. Each corner of the small triangles = 100% of the respective fuel component. The 1-hr and 10-hr fine fuels are combined on the lower left triangle so that the percentage of vegetation biomass (herbs and shrubs) can be included with the small fuels. The placement of a fuel bed on the upper diamond depends on where the composition falls within each of the two lower triangles. If all fuel within the bed consists of only duff, the dot for the bed falls on the extreme left of the lower triangle and is projected to the upper portion of the diamond along with the proportion of litter. Scale = 0 to 100% along each edge of the lower triangles and along each edge of the upper diamond.

B

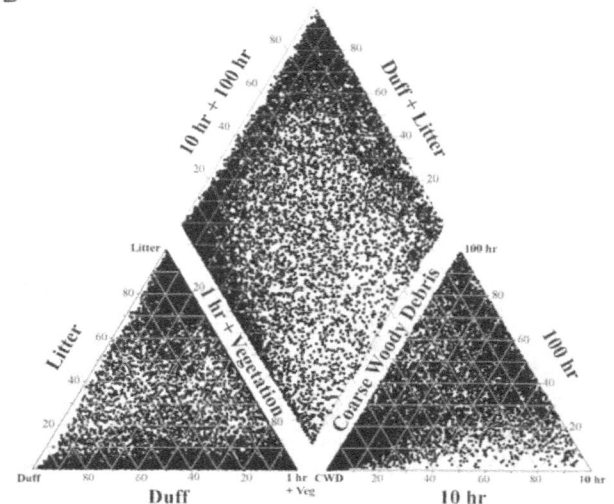

None of the fuel variables (Table 3) in the actual or synthetic data set were normally distributed, nor could they be made normally distributed with common transformations. Histograms for all eight fuel components were skewed to the left (i.e., concentrations of small values) and QQ plots were sigmoid in shape with long tails on each end. Histograms of data from the FOFEM outputs were also skewed to the left, although some had bimodal tendencies, and the QQ plots were sigmoid in shape with long tails on one or both ends. Correlation tests on the input data showed duff depth (DuffDep) and duff biomass (DuffBio) highly correlated with the 10-hr fuels and with each other. Correlations using the Spearman correlation were 0.87, 0.88, and 1.0 ($p < 0.0001$). Pearson's correlation tests on the standardized output from FOFEM simulation burning showed that S1 and SL60 were highly correlated (0.87) as were S5 and SL60 (0.86, $p < 0.0001$) and S1 and S5 (0.91, $p < 0.0001$). These variables showed significant differences, however, when tested among the individual moisture scenario runs using Kruskal-Wallis Chi-squared tests ($p < 0.0001$).

Of the ten FOFEM outputs used to measure intensity, time, and total consumption, almost all showed significant differences among the 10 moisture scenarios in both the actual and synthetic data sets ($p < 0.0001$). Only FIMax was not significantly different ($p < 0.55$). Some moisture scenarios had similar burn characteristics for the soil variables (SL60 and S1), but they were still different enough to be highly significant using the non-parametric ANOVA tests ($p < 0.001$).

Cluster Analysis

Based on distinct divisions within the dendrogram, we found that a classification of the synthetic dataset could contain two to 24 groups (Fig. 3). We found that the optimal number of groups ranged from four to 18 based on the Cubic Clustering Criterion, Pseudo-F, and Pseudo-t-squared tests. The clearest indication of the optimal number of groups came from the Pseudo-t-squared test, which indicated seven to nine groups would be most appropriate, but we experimented with classifications ranging from six to 14 groups. Ultimately, we chose nine groups to use for the surface fuels classification (see Fig. 3, line indicating 9-group level), because they separated well on the dendrogram's normal semi-partial R-squared value and could be differentiated on the basis of field characteristics for the fire and fuel beds. By determining why the dendrogram branched at each point (i.e., using means and ranges for each of the five analysis variables), we easily assigned differences in burn characteristics to nine groups; but found subsequent attempts at assigning surface fuel criteria to 14 groups using means and ranges was difficult (Fig. 3).

Means for the five FOFEM output variables used in the agglomerative clustering are shown by class in Table 4. Significant differences in the fire variables were found among the classes using Kruskal-Wallis non-parametric tests ($p < 0.0001$). The relationships between dendrogram branching and the five main fire effects used for the cluster process are shown in Figure 3. Along each branch of the dendrogram, the dominant pre-burn fuel characteristics for each of the nine classes are shown in Figure 4.

The characteristics for each of the nine cluster classes are summarized in Tables 5 and 6. The tables also include characteristics for additional fire effects from FOFEM outputs that were not used in the clustering process. The most important variables to class formation from the synthetic dataset were soil heating, fire intensity and burn time, and a combination of burn time and total consumption. Temperature in the top 1 cm (0.4 in) of the soil horizon and the total depth of heat

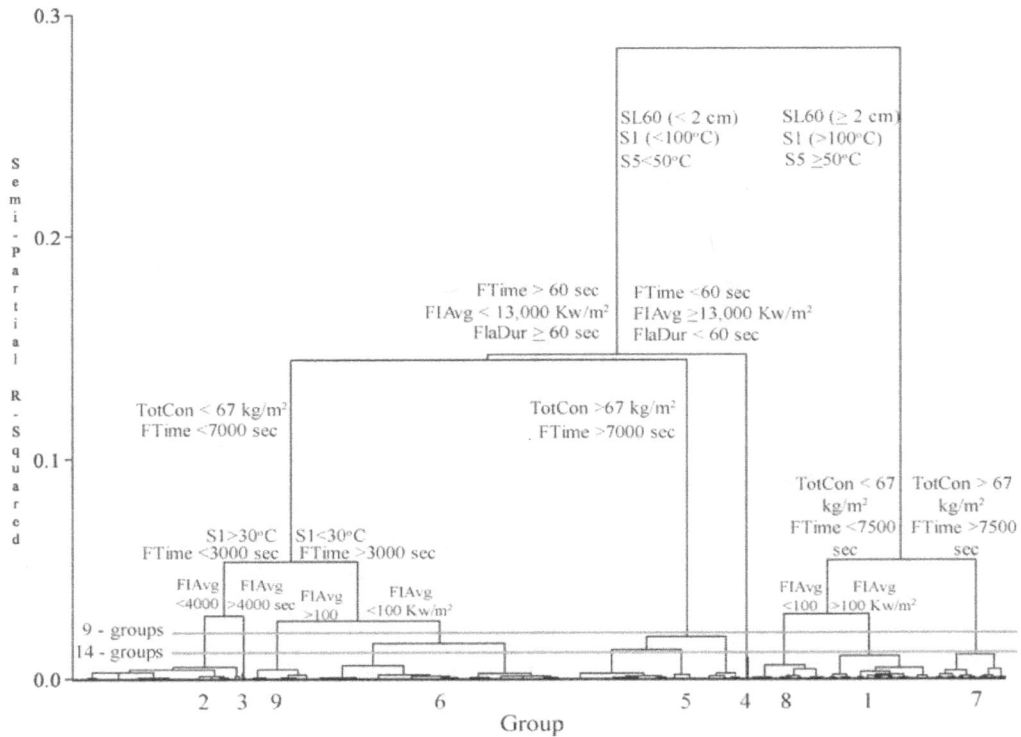

Figure 3—Dendrogram showing the groupings of synthetic fuel beds based on outputs from the simulation burns in FOFEM. The cluster was run using Ward's method and standardized variables for total fuels consumed (TotCon), average fire intensity (FIAvg), duration of fire (FTime), deepest soil layer to reach 60 °C (SL60), and maximum temperature reached at 1 cm below the surface (S1). Additional variables that distinguish groups include temperature of soil layer 5 centimeters below the surface (S5) and flame duration (FlaDur). Each branch is labeled with its dominant characteristic(s). Numerical values are means for each division. The 9-group and 14-group divisions are designated by horizontal lines. N = 115,280 fuel beds.

Table 4—Mean values (by class) of fire effects used in agglomerative clustering. The standard error for each mean is shown in parentheses. Differences among classes using the five variables were significant using Kruskal-Wallis tests (p < 0.0001).

CLUSTER or Class	n	Total fuels consumed (TotCon) kg m⁻²	Average fire intensity (FIAvg) Kw m⁻²	Soil depth reaching 60 °C (SL60) cm	Fire residence time (FTime) sec	Soil temp @ 1cm (S1) °C
1	12,664	40.29 (0.21)	156.81 (1.44)	5.46 (0.01)	3120.09 (12.49)	207.37 (0.54)
2	20,936	21.38 (0.12)	199.24 (2.18)	-0.44 (0.01)	1542.38 (7.02)	37.07 (0.15)
3	469	37.89 (1.01)	4518.43 (68.58)	0.89 (0.11)	74.87 (0.79)	75.59 (3.46)
4	264	55.16 (1.03)	13199.96 (237.60)	-0.02 (0.11)	62.16 (0.32)	47.19 (2.92)
5	22,468	86.15(0.19)	131.10 (0.33)	-0.18 (0.01)	7853.45 (2.55)	42.01 (0.22)
6	31,092	33.36 (0.08)	69.31 (0.27)	-0.68 (0.00)	5192.68 (9.30)	31.54 (0.10)
7	9,206	72.19 (0.33)	123.42 (0.52)	6.25 (0.02)	7438.45 (9.86)	215.44 (0.61)
8	9,877	31.70 (0.21)	94.00 (0.85)	2.53 (0.01)	3672.49 (16.09)	104.62 (0.29)
9	8,304	78.93 (0.18)	196.19 (1.47)	-0.84 (0.00)	3664.84 (17.81)	26.76 (0.13)

penetration that reached lethal limits for living tissue (i.e., 60 °C/140 °F) define classes early in the process, but they were also highly correlated with each other because both reflect heat conducted in the same soil horizon. Classes 1, 7, and 8 represented fuel beds that, when burned, resulted in an average predicted temperature >100 °C (212 °F) in the upper 1 cm of the soil surface and that reached lethal temperature for living tissue from 2 to 7 cm (0.75 to 2.75 in) deep (i.e., "deep burns"). Classes 2, 4, 5, 6 and 9 resulted from burns that did not reach lethal limits

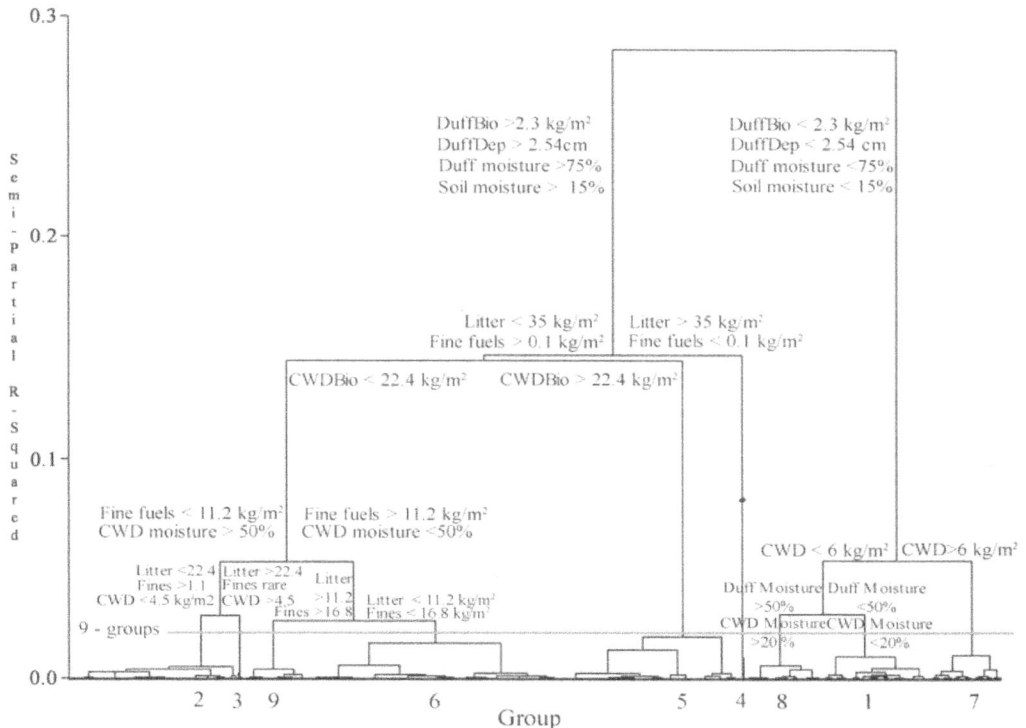

Figure 4—Dendrogram showing the groupings of synthetic fuel beds based on the original fuel characteristics of the cluster groups. The cluster was run using Ward's method and standardized variables for total fuels consumed (TotCon), average fire intensity (FIAvg), duration of fire (FTime), deepest soil layer to reach 60 °C (SL60), and maximum temperature reached at 1 cm below the surface (S1). Original fuels and moisture characteristics include: duff biomass (DuffBio), duff depth (DuffDep), coarse woody debris biomass (CWDBio), coarse woody debris moisture (CWD moisture), 1-hr + 10-hr + 100-hr grouped (Fine fuels), litter, and soil moisture. Each branch is labeled with the original fuel characteristic that is important to branching. Numerical values are based on means and range of values for each group. The nine-group division is designated by the horizontal line. N = 115,280.

for organics at more than 2 cm deep and did not create temperatures >75 °C (167 °F) in the upper 1 cm of soil (i.e., "shallow burns"). Classes 5 and 7 burned with relatively long duration (i.e., "Slow burns") while Classes 3 and 4 were characteristic of very short,"flashy" burns (Fig. 3, Table 5).

The mean fuel loads for each fuel type and the moisture conditions from the original fuel beds that correspond to each cluster class are summarized in Table 6. The range of loading values by fuel component and percent moisture values for each class are shown in Appendix A. Significant differences in fuel moistures and fuel compositions were found among all the cluster groups using Kruskal-Wallis non-parametric tests (p < 0.0001).

Visual examination of fuel bed distributions for three key fire variables shows that the clusters divide fairly well in three- dimensional space, although the sheer number of plots makes the distribution of some groups difficult to assess. Most groups are distinct (Fig. 5), but locating the full extent of Group 6 in the scatterplot is difficult. The scatterplot also shows that several of the groups span a range from shallow to deep burns within the same group, but others like Group 2 have a narrow range of burn depth (Fig. 5, lower center). Statistical summaries showed significant differences between the means of the five fire variables using Wilk's Lambda (p < 0.000) and highly correlated values for SL60 and S1 (>0.86).

The effects of moisture on the classification process were complex (Fig. 6). Each cluster class contained fuel beds from all moisture scenarios. Classes 1 and

Table 5—Median values for characteristics in each burn severity class based hierarchical clustering of the synthetic dataset using all moisture scenarios. Cluster classes are arranged in order of decreased soil heating. -1 = surface heating only.

Fire effect	7	1	8	3	2	5	4	6	9
Fuel consumed kg m^{-2} (t ac^{-1})	65.93 (294.1)	38.15 (170.2)	25.53 (113.9)	32.59 (145.4)	17.21 (76.8)	80.90 (360.9)	54.51 (243.2)	33.87 (151.1)	75.03 (334.7)
Soil depth that reached 60°C (cm)	6.0	5.0	3.0	-1	-1	-1	-1	-1	-1
Fire characteristic									
Soil heating upper 1 cm (°C)	209	201	101	41	28	22	20	20	20
Soil heating at 5cm (°C)	70	65	49	27	23	21	20	20	20
Fire intensity	116	115	72	4373	88	125	12839	58	153
Burn tme (sec)	7995	3225	3825	75	1485	7995	60	4875	3885
Flame duration (sec)	3180	1140	1095	60	300	3810	60	1185	1245
Smoke duration (sec)	24225	9975	10110	3795	7365	29430	4088	13890	17040

Table 6—Median values for original (pre-burn) fuel loads and moisture percentages by cluster group.

Fuel component	7	1	8	3	2	5	4	6	9
Duff biomass kg m^{-2} (t ac^{-1})	0.78 (3.5)	1.23 (5.48)	0.78 (3.5)	3.34 (14.9)	4.75 (21.2)	5.83 (26.0)	4.89 (21.8)	6.28 (28.0)	12.02 (53.6)
Duff depth cm (in)	0.34 (0.13)	0.54 (0.21)	0.34 (0.13)	1.50 (0.59)	2.10 (0.83)	2.60 (1.02)	2.20 (0.87)	2.80 (1.10)	5.40 (2.13)
Litter biomass kg m^{-2} (t ac^{-1})	4.46 (19.9)	5.85 (26.1)	1.95 (8.7)	21.86 (97.5)	1.39 (6.2)	8.14 (36.3)	46.52 (207.5)	1.43 (6.4)	41.31 (184.3)
Fine fuels biomass kg m^{-2} (t ac^{-1})	9.46 (42.2)	8.79 (39.2)	5.38 (24.0)	0.04 (0.17)	1.23 (5.5)	9.89 (44.1)	0.02 (0.1)	4.60 (20.5)	16.63 (74.2)
CWD biomass kg m^{-2} (t ac^{-1})	33.8 (150.8)	2.20 (9.8)	2.98 (13.3)	3.81 (17.0)	1.66 (7.4)	40.1 (178.9)	3.65 (16.3)	5.76 (25.7)	2.68 (11.9)
Moisture (%)									
Duff	40	40	50	75	100	100	75	100	100
10H	8	6	8	8	8	8	8	8	8
CWD	15	15	20	40	20	20	40	20	20
Soil	10	10	10	20	20	15	20	15	1

7 had the most fuel beds burned under the driest moisture scenario (A). The most fuel beds from wettest scenarios (F and I) were found in clusters 2, 5, and 6. Class 5 and 9 had approximately equal representation of all moisture scenarios; whereas the number of fuel beds burned under each scenario varied considerably within classes 1, 2, 6, and 7. Of the 10 moisture scenarios created for this study, two were almost identical in their maximum, minimum, and mean values for all of the FOFEM outputs (i.e., scenarios D and H). Two other pairs (G and J; and F and I) were so similar that we considered eliminating one of each pair to run subsequent statistical analyses. However, Kruskal-Wallis comparisons showed significant differences among all the scenarios so we retained all of them.

The effect of fuel and soil moistures on depth of burn, fuel consumed, and smoke duration is shown in Fig. 6. Moisture scenario A, which is the driest scenario, had the deepest burns and high fuel consumption. The wettest scenarios (H and I)

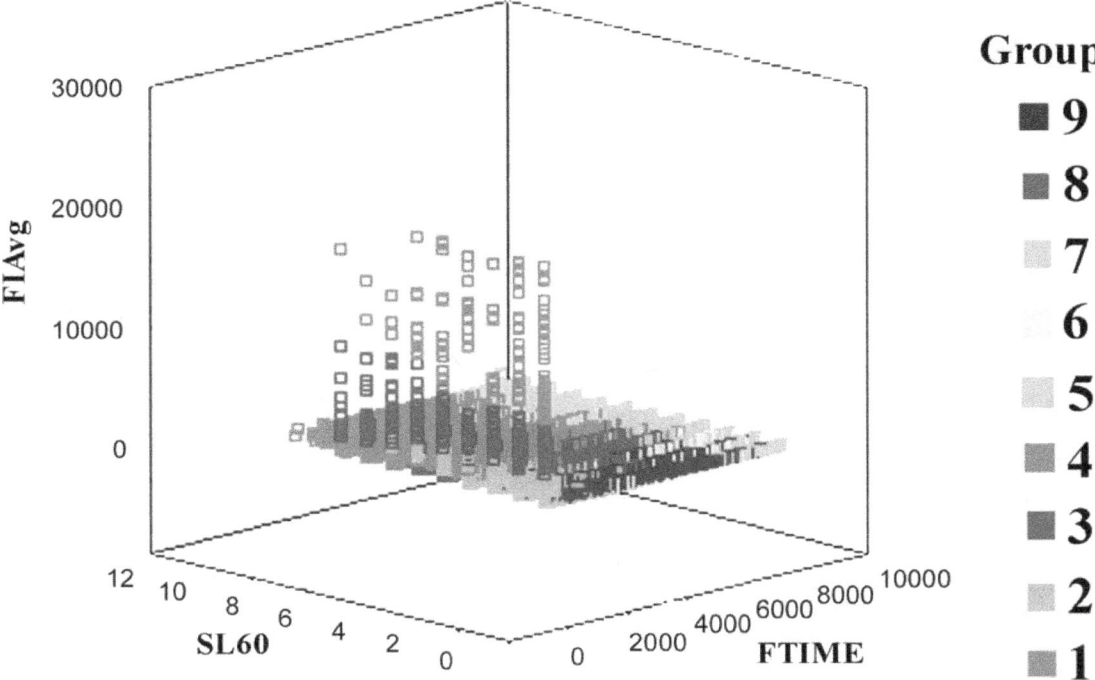

Figure 5—Scatterplot of group distributions for the three variables explaining the most variation in the synthetic data set (FIAvg = 46.9%; FTime = 27.6%; SL60 = 19.4%). Groups were created by agglomerative clustering. The most variation in fire intensity occurs within groups 2, 3, and 4. Plot shows results from simulation burning of all fuel beds in all moisture scenarios (n = 115,280). FIAvg = average fire intensity (KW m^{-2}), SL60 = soil depth (cm) that reaches 60°C, FTime = fire duration (sec).

predicted shallow burns and longer smoke durations for those fuels that could burn (i.e., depth >-1). Clusters 2 and 6 consistently plotted with shallow burn depths, low fuel consumption, and moderate smoke. Clusters 1, 7, 8, which predicted long, deep burns in cluster analysis (Fig. 3), consistently occurred in the upper portion of each moisture scenario but the amount of fuel consumed resulted in different spreads for the groups (Fig. 6 above 2 cm depth of burn). Scenarios with moist fuels and soil predicted little consumption but longer smoke if more fuels were consumed. Scenario E was perhaps the most interesting because all cluster groups were spread out along all three axes.

Class Verification

The uniqueness and consistency of the nine classes produced from the synthetic dataset was verified using three methods: cluster analysis of an independent dataset (i.e., the actual dataset), classification and regression tree analysis (CART), and discriminant analysis (DA).

Verification Using an Actual Dataset

Agglomerative hierarchical clustering of the actual data set showed the same general branching patterns in the dendrogram as the synthetic data set. Both the synthetic and actual data sets had classes at the far right and left sides of the dendrogram to create the difference between six and nine groups (Fig. 7). Initial clusters were divided on the same soil temperatures and burn depth variables as the synthetic data set. Subsequent divisions were also similar to synthetic data set, but the actual data set had much lower average fire intensities and total consumption

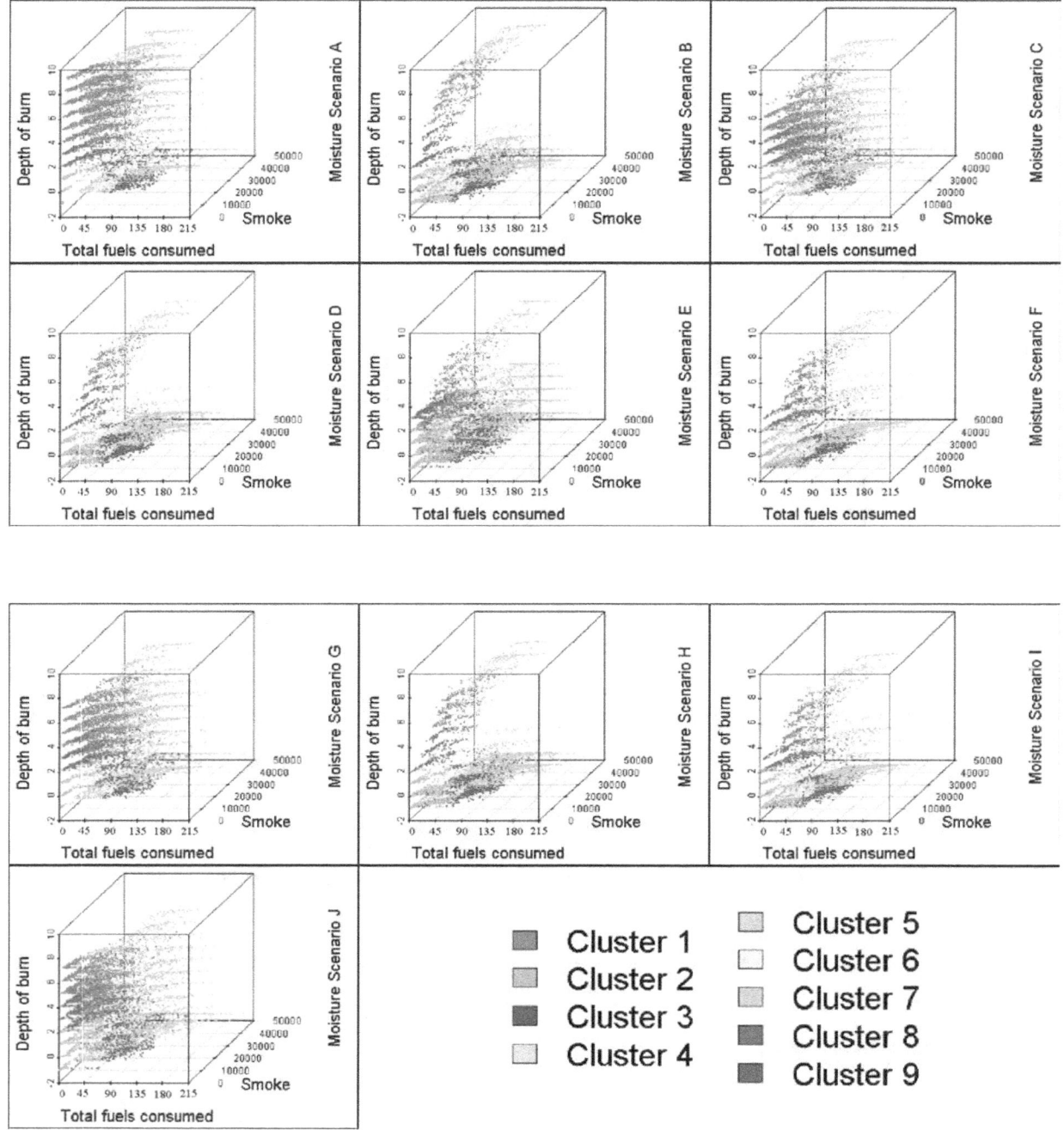

Figure 6—Scatterplots showing the variation in total consumed (kg m^{-2}), depth of burn (cm), and smoke duration (seconds) for the 10 moisture scenarios described in Table 2 (n = 11528 fuel beds for each scenario). Each cluster is color coded to show the variation in abundance of fuelbeds from each group. Each moisture scenario contains members from all clusters. Kruskal-Wallis comparisons showed the moisture scenarios to be significantly different (p < 0.0001). For the three variables shown in these scatterplots, all were also significantly different among the scenarios (Kruskal-Wallis p < 0.0001). Surface burns are at 0 on the depth of burn axes and -1 indicates no burn.

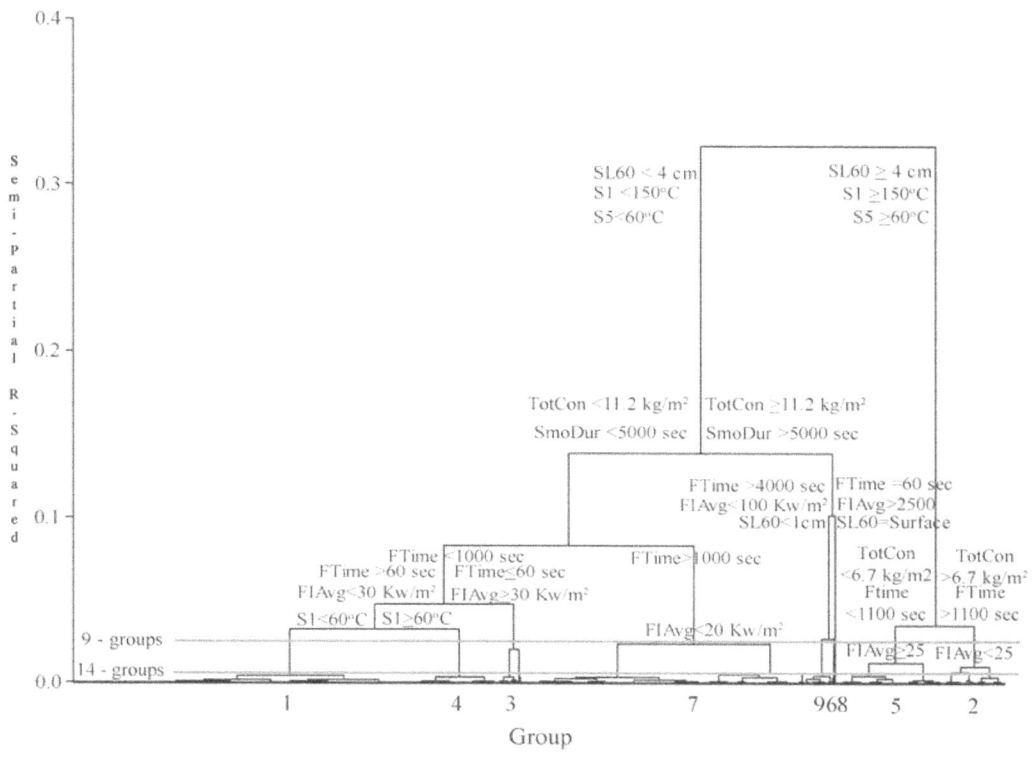

Figure 7—Dendrogram showing the groupings of the actual fuel beds based on outputs from the simulation burns in FOFEM. The cluster was run using Ward's method and standardized variables for total fuels consumed (TotCon), average fire intensity (FIAvg), duration of fire (FTime), deepest soil layer to reach 60 °C (SL60), and maximum temperature reached at 1 cm below the surface (S1). Additional variables that distinguish groups include temperature of soil layer 5 centimeters below the surface (S5) and smoke duration (SmoDur). Each branch is labeled with its dominant characteristic(s). Numerical values are means for each division. The 9-group and 14-group divisions are designated by the horizontal lines. N = 115,280.

values because the ranges of fuel loading were more restricted. The main differences between the classification created with the actual data set and the synthetic data set occurred within the "deep burn" groups (right side of dendrogram, Fig. 3) where the actual field data contained only 1/10 of the surface fuels for total consumption and fire times differed by ½ to ¾ that of the synthetic data set. Smoke duration was also important to dendrogram branching earlier in the actual data set than in the synthetic data set.

Verification with Classification and Regression Tree Analysis (CART)

CART split the burned fuel beds based on the standardized fire effect outputs differently than cluster analysis. Where depth of soil heating was most important in cluster analysis, fire time (FTime) was most important in CART for dividing the actual and synthetic data sets. For the synthetic data set, the difference between short- and long-burning fires created the initial split in classes (Fig. 8b); soil heating, either in the top 1 cm (0.4 in) of the soil horizon (Z_S1, right branch, Fig. 8) or in the depth of the soil horizon that reached lethal temperatures (Z-SL60, left branch, Fig. 8), was of secondary importance. In CART analysis of the synthetic data set, Classes 3 and 4 were not distinguished; both were characterized by few fuel beds in comparison to other groups and very high average fire intensities. CART analysis of both data sets also resulted in several classes (Classes 2,3,5,6 and 7) being duplicated on opposite branches of the regression tree (Fig. 8). The

A

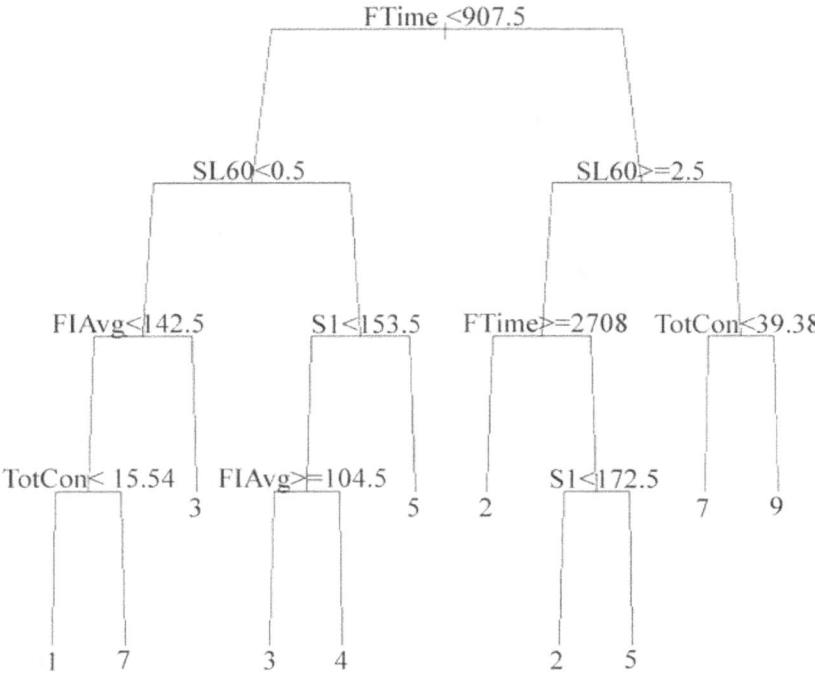

B

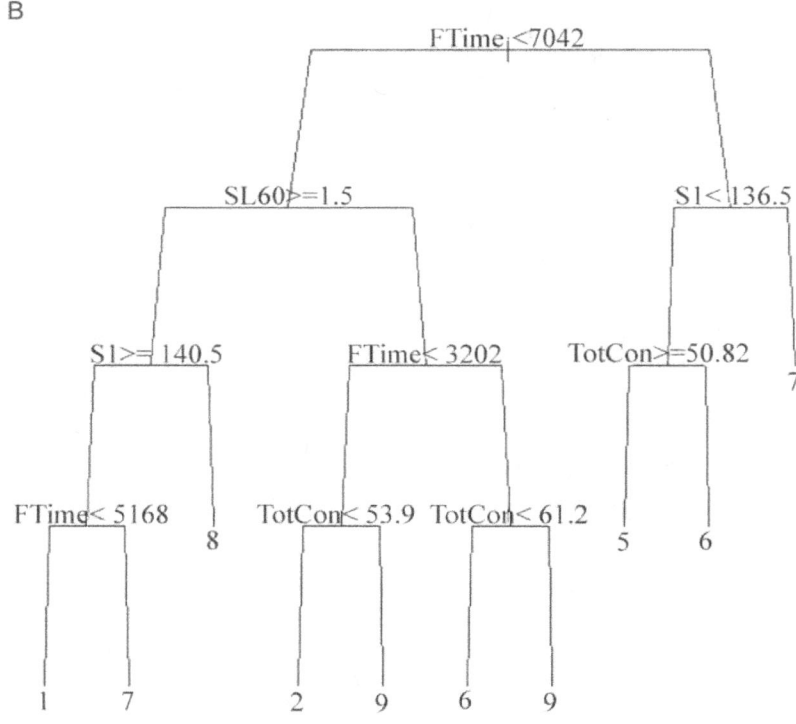

Figure 8—Classification and regression trees based on the nine classes created during hierarchical cluster analysis (A) actual data set (B) synthetic data set. Variables included total fuels consumed (TotCon) in kg m^{-2}, fire time (FTime) in sec, temperature 1 cm (0.4 in) below the soil surface (S1) in °C, deepest soil depth (SL60) to reach 60 °C (140 °F) in cm, and the average fire intensity achieved during the burn (FIAvg) in Kw m^{-2}. Standardized values of each variable were used in the analysis but the corresponding raw values were used as labels in this illustration. Terminal nodes are labeled with the class value from hierarchical agglomerative clustering.

splits based on FTime failed to uniquely assign individual results to one single class within the synthetic data set because fuel beds on both sides of the first CART split burned for longer than 7,042 sec. Within R, the pruning rules for the CART tree required that the minimum number of observations in a node be 30 before a split is attempted and the split must decrease the overall lack of fit by 0.001. All of the classes from the cluster analysis had over 30 observations (Table 4).

Verification with Discriminant Analysis

Statistical summaries showed significant differences between the means of the five fire variables using Wilk's Lambda ($p < 0.0001$) and highly correlated values for SL60 and S1 (>0.86). Five canonical discriminant functions showed how much variation in the data was explained by each of the fire variables. The first canonical discriminant function, and the most important, related to FIAvg. It had a canonical correlation (CC) of 0.935 and explained 46.9% of the variation in the data. The other significant canonical discrimination functions, in decreasing explanatory order, were FTime (CC 0.896 explaining 27.6% of the variation), SL60 (CC 0.860, 19.4%), TotCon (CC 0.687, 6.1%), and S1 (CC 0.058, 0%). Of the original groupings found in cluster analysis, 97.9% were classified in the same groups using discriminant analysis resubstitution; 97.7% of fuel beds classified in the same groups as cluster analysis using discriminant analysis cross-validation (Table 7). The class with the greatest error in assignments was Class 2 (8.82%); classes 3, 4, 7, and 9 all classified with <1% error compared to the cluster groups.

Table 7—Classification results from non-parametric discriminant analysis using standardized values for total consumed (TotCon), average fire intensity (FIAvg), fire time (FTime), maximum temperature in the upper 1-cm soil horizon (S1), and depth that reached 60 °C in subsurface (SL60).

Tests of equality of the group means for these five variables using Wilkes Lambda showed the means were significantly different ($p < 0.000$). Eigenvalues for the first five canonical discriminant functions were 6.9 (explaining 46.9% of variance), 4.0 (27.6%), 2.85 (19.4%), 0.895 (6.1%) and 0.003 (0%), respectively.

		Predicted group membership using non-parametric discriminant analysis (percent)									
	CLUSTER	1	2	3	4	5	6	7	8	9	Total
Re-substituted [a]	1	**98.18**	0	0	0	0	0	0.43	1.39	0	100
	2	0	**97.13**	0.02	0	0	1.04	0	0.91	0.89	100
	3	0	0	**100**	0	0	0	0	0	0	100
	4	0	0	0	**100**	0	0	0	0	0	100
	5	0.06	0	0	0	**97.42**	0.22	0.47	0.64	1.19	100
	6	0	3.12	0	0	1.62	**91.23**	0	0.84	3.19	100
	7	0.26	0	0	0	0	0	**99.73**	0.01	0	100
	8	0.35	0.06	0	0	0.05	0	0.12	**99.09**	0.32	100
	9	0	0.04	0	0	0.58	0.01	0	0.19	**99.18**	100
	Total	10.85	18.49	0.41	0.23	19.47	24.84	8.11	9.18	8.43	100
	Error[d]	1.82	2.87	0	0	2.58	8.77	0.27	0.91	0.82	2.01
Cross-validated [b, c]	1	**97.58**	0.01	0	0	0.02	0	0.74	1.65	0	100
	2	0.03	**96.99**	0.04	0	0	1.05	0	0.96	0.93	100
	3	0	0.64	**99.15**	0.21	0	0	0	0	0	100
	4	0	0	0	**100**	0	0	0	0	0	100
	5	0.07	0	0	0	**97.25**	0.23	0.53	0.71	1.22	100
	6	0	3.12	0	0	1.64	**91.18**	0	0.86	3.19	100
	7	0.51	0	0	0	0.04	0	**99.44**	0.01	0	100
	8	0.57	0.09	0	0	0.05	0	0.13	**98.79**	0.37	100
	9	0	0.06	0	0	0.58	0.01	0	0.29	**99.06**	100
	Total	10.83	18.47	0.41	0.23	19.45	24.83	8.14	9.21	8.44	100
	Error[d]	2.42	3.01	0.85	0	2.75	8.82	0.56	1.21	0.94	2.29

[a] 97.99% of re-substituted cases correctly classified.

[b] 97.71% of cross-validated grouped cases correctly classified.

[c] Cross validation is done only for those cases in the analysis. In cross validation, each case is classified by the functions derived from all cases other than that case.

[d] Error count estimates for classification variable (rate) expressed as percent.

Summary of Validation Results

The results of the three validation methods can be summarized as follows:

1) The synthetic and actual datasets produced the same number of classes (Figs. 3, 7).

2) Even though the actual dataset had fuel beds with less than half the biomass for each fuel component than the synthetic dataset, the clustering dendrogram showed essentially that the same fire variables were important to each major branch and at similar levels in the dendrogram. The limited ranges in biomass values resulted in lower temperatures and burn times that mainly affected the labeling of split branches more than the actual order or differences variable importance (Fig. 7).

3) CART created classes of fire severity based first on fire time (FTIME), which made comparison with methods that split first on soil heating (S60 and S1) difficult (Figs. 3, 8).

4) CART created 10 (11 in actual dataset) classes, but some of the classes were duplicated on opposing branches of the regression tree (i.e., Class 6) and Classes 3 and 4 were missing altogether (Fig. 8). Separation of Classes 1, 8, and 9 was incomplete because each of these groups contained fuel beds with fire times greater than 7,042 seconds but the groups reside only on the left side of the diagrams where fire times were less than 7,042 sec.

5) Discriminant analysis produced similar results to hierarchical clustering, but Class 6 had 8.82% classification error and Classes 2 and 5 each had approximately 3% of their total fuel beds misclassified (Table 7).

Discussion

We successfully created a fire severity classification that merged fire effects from surface fuel loadings with associated fire behavior for a wide range of moisture conditions. Using a classification process based on empirical data, the variance inherent in over 115,000 very different fuel beds was objectively distributed among nine unique, identifiable groups. Fuel beds were correctly placed into the nine fire severity classes 98% of the time using subsets of the synthetic fuel beds (Table 7) and independently verified using fuel loading data from real fuel beds (Fig. 7). More importantly, the classification seems to uniquely identify these classes in ways that are important to planning and management (Tables 5, 6) and presents groups of fire effects and fire behaviors that are realistically different and meaningful (Fig. 3, 4). Even though the classification was created with computer simulation, the creation of unique, realistic, and reproducible classes gave us confidence that the classes would be useful predictors of fire severity from on-site fuels.

Evaluation of the Fire Severity Classification Process

Our main objective in this study was to present a methodology to create an objective fire severity classification based on fire behavior and effects that would represent loadings and combustion across a wide diversity of fuel beds and improve predictability of fire effects. We found this process to be quite straightforward: (1) find or create a large number of fuel beds, (2) find a mechanism to burn them, (3) group the fuel beds together by the outputs they have in common, and (4) find a method to verify that the classes are uniquely identified and consistent.

Burning the real and synthetic fuel beds was the most problematic step in the classification process because the actual burning of so many diverse fuel beds on the landscape is impractical. Measuring effects that result from burning different vegetation types can also be problematic because each effect requires a different measurement during an actual burn. For example, measuring how deep a fire affects in the soil horizon during burning would require one set of instrumentation but measuring fire residence time in the different fuel components would require quite another. For most fires, collecting these measurements and relating them to the physical properties of the fire is time consuming, costly, and labor intensive. During the past four decades, significant progress has been made in the development of fire models that more realistically describe the physical aspects of fire and predict how different types of fuel beds burn (Anderson et al. 2006; Andrews 1986; Finney 2004; Parsons et al. 2011; Reinhardt and Keane 1998). These models make the simulation of fuel bed combustion more practical than using actual fire on the landscape and have paved the way for creating a basic classification based solely on fuels.

The main problems with the current burn simulation models is that (1) they have no spatial context that would vary fire effects based on the spatial arrangement of fuels on the ground (Reinhardt et al. 1997); (2) they cannot incorporate topography or wind, both of which are crucial to realistic fire severity values on the surface and in the soil; and (3) FOFEM, in particular, has been shown to underestimate duff consumption and fireline intensity in some fuel types (Hood et al. 2007). That said, it is more practical to simulate fuel bed combustion with these limited models than to use fire on the landscape to burn the large number of fuel beds needed to create an adequate classification that covers numerous possibilities of fuel components and moisture combinations. Moreover, our severity classification is "tuned" to FOFEM, which means that we can approximate likely fire severity prior to burning using FOFEM if we can know or estimate likely fuel and soil moistures.

Grouping fire behavior and fire effects variables from burn simulations under different moisture scenarios was straightforward using the agglomerative hierarchical clustering. It was also the most objective method for grouping because it assured that the number of groups was determined by the similarities in the data and not by operator bias. The number of classes used for this study could easily have ranged from six to 20 based on the cluster optimization tests, but our analyses ultimately led us to a nine-group surface fuel classification that best represented several different types of fires and was also relevant to fire effects that can be observed in the field. Constructing a classification based on more than nine classes was much more difficult because unique fire effects, intensities, and fire times were difficult if not impossible to distinguish between groups (Figs. 3, 4). Plotting the fuel beds by fire effect showed the same groups identified with cluster analysis plotting together on the scatterplot (Fig. 6) and the fire effects predicted within each scenario seemed reasonable. For example, very dry scenario A burned deeper and consumed more fuel than the wetter I or J scenarios, which had much less fuel consumed and often did not burn (i.e., depth of burn = -1).

Validating the classes proved to be challenging because the three different methods produced three different results, although the differences among techniques were not as great as expected. Some of the differences in verification results can be explained by the way the individual classification processes run. CART and DA use different approaches to dividing groups (McCune and Grace 2002). The missing classes 3 and 4 in CART and the arrangement of the tree could be due to either the stopping rules (clusters 3 and 4 have small numbers of samples) or pruning rules that are based on the variability within and between groups or how much classification error remains. Why CART separated the fuel beds on fire time instead of depth of burned like the hierarchical clustering is not known for certain (order of variables was not a factor). Theoretically, fire time and depth of burn should be highly correlated, and we did find them significantly correlated with correlation analysis (Pearson correlation coefficient = 0.04, $p < 0.0001$). We also found FTime highly correlated with fire temperatures at depth (S1 and S5, $p < 0.0001$). Because soil heating and depth of burn are rate-limited processes, duration of burning or fire time should be much more important to creating fire effects than fire intensity, which make the CART classes additively informative to our fire severity classification.

Limitations of the Classification and Suggestions to Improve Predictability

Our classification can be compared only generally to other fire severity classifications that quantitatively describe fire effects in the soil horizon. Feller's (1998) low fire severity classes from slash burning would correspond to the depths of burn <2 cm (0.75 in) on the left side of our dendrogram (Fig. 3). All of Feller's other classes (moderate to very high) fall within the deeper burns on the right side of the dendrogram (classes 1, 7, and 8). There was no one-to-one correspondence between his classification and ours. The classes developed by Trowbridge et al. (1989) using duff depth and total consumption of slash fuels are not readily comparable to the biomass and consumption values for each fuel bed in our classification. Trowbridge et al. (1989) used a maximum of duff consumed; our classification focuses on the depth of the original duff and what fire effects burning that thickness of duff would cause. Both Trowbridge et al. (1989) and Feller (1988) focused on fire effects from burning slash piles. Our classification is based on a much broader range of fuel components and focuses on the diverse fuel types that would be found throughout the United States.

While the presented classification can be used in the field in its current form, there are several limitations that must be addressed when it is used. First, most forest and non-forest *surface* fuels are represented within this classification by size or origins, not by specific genera or species composition (e.g., feather moss, lichen, pine-needles or grass are not specifically incorporated in the fuel beds but may be considered as part of the herb or, when dried, litter classes). The classification does not, incorporate any tree *canopy fuels* or their associated fire effects into its design and it should not be used to predict fire severity within the canopy or tree strata. Second, although we feel that the fire variables used to construct the classification span the vital characteristics in fuel consumption—fire time and soil effects—we may have limited its usefulness by using only five fire variables and excluding other fire effects in its construction. Our rationale for excluding several FOFEM outputs, which we did explore during this process, was that these five showed the most promise for field applications and providing ecological differences. The effect of this decision can be tested in future work by classifying the datasets using predictors other than these five and comparing the results. Third, the BURNUP model in FOFEM used to simulate fuel bed combustion may inaccurately portray some combustion dynamics for simulated data because the fuel characteristics may be outside the limits of its algorithms or the model assumptions. The duff consumption model is particularly problematic and needs refinement in all fire models that use its algorithms. Carefully planned experiments in the lab or field to solve the thin-duff/heat insulator problem and the deep duff effects are critical to creating a better classification. Finally, managers who use this classification should be aware that the class characteristics will greatly benefit from verification. Verification will require measuring pre-burn fuel beds; then recording temperatures during the burn, fuel consumption, and fire effects at the exact points where the fuels were measured. Although it is impractical to observe the large number of fuel beds and range of fires represented within this classification due to economic, logistical, and methodological constraints, a class or subset of each group could be tested in the laboratory or field to verify our class characteristics. Because this classification is based on physical properties of fire, it can be explored or tested with carefully planned experiments and, to a limited extent, in the field to determine if the classes created with computer simulation reasonably reflect the fire effects for different intensities of fire or if they need refinement to match real situations. Such experiments would also inform development of improved models linking fire behavior to fire effects, particularly if observations were spatially explicit and captured spatial heterogeneity in fuels and fires.

Ultimately, this classification represents the most complete, objective, empirical integration of fuels, moisture effects, and fire characteristics to date. It is most useful as a tool for predicting fire severity from pre-burn fuels and moisture conditions. Exceptions to its use may be fuel beds with extremely thin or extremely thick duff that FOFEM may not model adequately at this time. Furthermore, this classification is not meant to be used in a post-burn environment where burning has destroyed surface fuels. Sometimes pre-fire conditions can be assessed from un-burned areas within the burn, or areas adjacent to the burn, to provide insight into fuel consumption, soil heating, and fire intensity. Other times, indices from other studies can be used in conjunction with this classification to estimate how severely fire has affected parts of the landscape. Jain et al. (2012) have summarized some of the indices that can be used in a post-burn environment to estimate fire severity effects in the soil and on trees. Additional work will be needed to tie predicted with actual post-burn effects using experiments or prescribed burns as described above.

Summary

The future of fire severity work will lie in quantitative studies that extend the same classification procedure used with the surface fuels (i.e., create fuels, burn them, classify the effects, and verify classes) to other biotic and abiotic components to form a complete picture of fire severity. In addition to the surface fuels, tree canopy consumption is an important fuel source that will need to be quantified. Physical effects due to the combustion process, such as ash production or nutrient changes, will also need to be quantified to create another piece of the fire severity picture. The physical properties of each of these types of fuels (e.g., their moisture content, depth, biomass, size and shape), biotic and abiotic characteristics, and the physical properties of the fire resulting from combinations of these fuels and biota burning on the landscape, have relationships that are observable, testable, and, ultimately, predictable. Exploring these relationships in quantitative terms presents one direction for future work in burn severity classification. Just as fire intensity, spread rates, and flame lengths are physical measures that have made fire behavior models more realistic, we feel that fire ecology critically needs a set of quantitative variables that describe fire effects in terms of the physical characteristics of a fire's effect to make fire severity classifications more realistic and versatile. Consider, for example, how much more versatile percent tree mortality is to relate to fire characteristics like intensity or flame duration than a fire severity category of low, medium, or high. Quantitative values more effectively link fire effects to the flaming and smoldering combustion processes represented in models that link fire behavior and effects. Likewise, we need variables that are ecologically meaningful and that we can readily measure at multiple scales remotely and in the field (Hudak et al. 2007; Lentile et al. 2006, 2007). Addressing the issue of variability of burns and how that affects fire severity classes across those spatial scales will take an integrated approach by many fields of science, including soils, geology, forestry, and remote sensing, among others. The proposed classification is an important step toward describing the mechanisms of fire severity that can provide the flexibility needed for use across multiple scales, applications, and projects.

According to Ryan and Noste (1985), a fire severity classification should possess several key attributes. It should be (1) a meaningful index of ecological change; (2) broadly applicable; (3) useful for predicting fire effects moderately accurately; (4) applicable to all types of fires; (5) applicable to many vegetation types; (6) easy to use; (7) safely implemented (i.e., with post-fire observations); and (8) easy for managers, scientists, and others to compare and evaluate field observations with predicted results. The classification created in this study meets most of these criteria, with the possible exception of being applicable to all types of fires. It is not meant to apply to crown fires in forests, but it could be expanded to do so in the future using a similar developmental process to this surface fuel fire severity classification. Like the fire severity rating system created by Ryan and Noste (1985), this surface-fuel classification integrates pre-fire conditions, fire behavior, and fire effects. However, it adds new dimension to the classifications previously developed by Ryan and Noste (1985), Feller (1998), and Trowbridge et al. (1989) because it places quantitative values on the fuels, moistures, and fire characteristics needed to produce specific fire effects. Its real strength is in the assessment of potential fire effects from pre-burn fuel variability and exploring the physical relationships with fire. Ultimately, it is just one step toward a more quantitative, objective, scalable approach to predicting fire severity from very accessible data, that is, the surface fuels and other on-site parameters.

References

Albini, Frank A. 1976. Computer based models of wildland fire behavior: a user's manual. Ogden, UT: U.S. Department of Agriculture, Forest Service, Intermountain Forest and Range Experiment Station. 68 p.

Albini, Frank A. 1994. Program burnup: A simulation model of the burning of large woody natural fuels. Final report on research grant INT-92754-GR. Bozeman, MT: U.S. Department of Agriculture, Forest Service, Intermountain Reseach Station. 111 p.

Albini, Frank A.; Reinhardt, Elizabeth D. 1995. Modeling ignition and burning rate of large woody natural fuels. International Journal of Wildland Fire. 5(2): 81-91.

Anderson, Gary; Ottmar, Roger D.; Prichard, Susan 2006. CONSUME. Seattle, WA: U.S. Department of Agriculture, Forest Service, Pacific Northwest Research Station, Pacific Wildland Fire Sciences Laboratory; Boise, ID: Hoefler Consulting Group.

Anderson, Hal E. 1982. Aids to determining fuel models for estimating fire behavior. INT-122. Ogden, UT: U.S. Department Agriculture, Forest Service, Intermountain Forest and Range Research Station. 22 p.

Andrews, P.L. 1986. BEHAVE: Fire behavior prediction and fuel modeling system. Gen. Tech. Rep. INT-194. Ogden, UT: U.S. Department of Agriculture, Forest Service, Intermountain Research Station. 130 p.

Azuma, David L.; Donnegan, J; Gedney, D. 2004. Southwestern Oregon's Biscuit fire: An analysis of forest resources and fire severity. Res. Pap. PNW-RP-560. Portland, OR: U.S. Department of Agriculture, Forest Service, Pacific Northwest Research Station. 32 p.

Beschta, Robert L.; Rhodes, Jonathan J.; Kauffman, J. Boone; [and others]. 2004. Postfire management on forested public lands of the western United States. Conservation Biology. 18(4): 957-967.

Boby, Leslie A.; Schuur, Edward A.G.; Mack, Michelle C.; [and others]. 2010. Quantifying fire severity, carbon, and nitrogen emissions in Alaska's boreal forest. Ecological Applications. 20(6): 1633-1647.

Boer, Matthias M.; Macfarlane, Craig; Norris, Jaymie; [and others]. 2008. Mapping burned areas and burn severity patterns in SW Australian eucalypt forest using remotely-sensed changes in leaf area index. Remote Sensing of Environment. 112(12): 4358-4369.

Bradley, Anne F.; Fischer, W.C.; Noste, N.V. 1992. Fire ecology of forest habitat types of eastern Idaho and western Wyoming. Gen. Tech Rep. INT-290. U.S. Department of Agriculture, Forest Service, Intermountain Forest and Range Experiment Station. 92 p.

Brown, J.K.; DeByle, Norbert V. 1987. Fire damage, mortality, and suckering in aspen. Canadian Journal of Forest Research. 17: 1100-1109.

Brown, James K.; Marsden, M.A.; Ryan, Kevin C.; Reinhardt, Elizabeth D. 1985. Predicting duff and woody fuel consumed by prescribed fire in the Northern Rocky Mountains. Res. Pap. INT-337. Ogden, UT: U.S. Department of Agriculture, Forest Service, Intermountain Forest and Range Experiment Station. 23 p.

Brumby, Steven P.; Harvey, Neal R.; Bloch, Jeffrey J.; [and others]. 2001. Evolving forest fire burn severity classification algorithms for multi-spectral imagery. Los Alamos, NM: Space and Remote Sensing Sciences, Los Alamos National Library. 10 p.

Byram, George M.; Nelson, R.M. 1952. Lethal temperatures and fire injury. Res. Note No. 1. Asheville, NC: U.S. Department of Agriculture, Forest Service, Southeastern Forest Experiment Station. 2 p.

Carey, Amanda; Evans, Murray; Hann, Peter; [and others]. 2003. Wildfires in the ACT 2003: Report on initial impacts on natural ecosystems. Tech. Rep. 17. Canberra: Australian Capital Territory. 94 p.

Chuvieco, E. 1999. Measuring changes in landscape pattern from satellite images: Short-term effects of fire on spatial diversity. International Journal of Remote Sensing. 20(12): 2331-2346.

De Santis, Angela; Chuvieco, Emilio. 2007. Burn severity estimation from remotely sensed data: Performance of simulation versus empirical models. Remote Sensing of Environment. 108: 422-435.

Díaz-Delgado, R.; Lloret, F. ; Pons, X. 2003. Influence of fire severity on plant regeneration through remote sensing imagery. International Journal of Remote Sensing. 24(8): 1751-1763.

Dillon, Gregory K.; Holden, Zachery A.; Morgan, Penelope; [and others]. 2011. Both topography and climate affected forest and woodland burn severity in two regions of the western US, 1984 to 2006. Ecosphere. 2(12): 130.

Epting, Justin; Verbyla, David; Sorbel, Brian. 2005. Evaluation of remotely sensed indices for assessing burn severity in interior Alaska using Landsat TM and ETM+. Remote Sensing of Enviroment. 96: 328-339.

Feller, M.C. 1988. Relationships between fuel properties and slashburning-induced nutrient losses. Forest Science. 34(4): 998-1015.

Feller, M.C. 1998. The influence of fire severity, not fire intensity, on understory vegetation biomass in British Columbia. In: 13th Fire and Forest Meteorology Conference; Oct. 27-31,1996; Lorne, Australia. International Association of Wildland Fire: 335-347.

Finney, Mark A. 2004. FARSITE: Fire Area Simulator: Model development and evaluation. Res. Pap. RMRS-RP-4. Ogden, UT: U.S. Department of Agriculture, Forest Service, Rocky Mountain Research Station. 47 p.

Foote, M. Joan. 1983. Classification, description, and dynamics of plant communities after fire in the tiaga of interior Alaska. Res. Pap. PNW-307. Portland, OR: U.S. Department of Agriculture, Forest Service, Pacific Northwest Forest and Range Experiment Station. 108 p.

Fosberg, M.A. 1970. Drying rates of heartwood below fiber saturation. Forest Science. 16: 57-63.

Heyerdahl, Emily K.; Lertzman, Ken; Wong, Carmen M. 2012. Mixed-severity fire regimes in dry forests of southern interior British Columbia, Canada. Canadian Journal of Forest Research. 42: 88-98.

Hood, Sharon M.; HcHugh, Charles W.; Ryan, Kevin C.; [and others]. 2007. Evaluation of a post-fire tree mortality model for western USA conifers. International Journal of Wildland Fire. 16: 679-689.

Hudak, Andrew T.; Morgan, Penelope; Bobbitt, Michael J.; [and others]. 2007. The relationship of multispectral satellite imagery to immediate fire effects. Fire Ecology. 3(1): 64-90.

Huffman, Edward L.; MacDonald, Lee H.; Stednick, John D. 2001. Strength and persistence of fire-induced soil hydrophobicity under ponderosa and lodgepole pine, Colorado, Front Range. Hydrological Processes. 15: 2877-2892.

Hungerford, R.D. 1996. Soils. Marana, AZ: U.S. Department of Agriculture, Forest Service, National Advanced Resouce Technology Center.

Jain, Theresa B. 2004. Tongue-tied. Wildfire. Birmingham, AL: International Association Wildland Fire(July/August): 22-26.

Jain, Theresa B.; Graham, Russell T. 2007. The relation between tree burn severity and forest structure in the Rocky Mountains. In: Powers, Robert F., ed., 2005 National Siliviculture Workshop; 6-10 June 2005; Tahoe City, CA. Gen. Tech. Rep. PSW-GTR-203. Albany, CA: U.S. Department of Agriculture, Forest Service, Pacific Southwest Research Station: 213-250.

Jain, Theresa B.; Graham, Russell T.; Pilliod, David S. 2006. The relation between forest structure and soil burn severity. In: Andrews, Patricia L.; Butler, Bret W., comps. Fuels Management—How to Measure Success; Conference Proceedings; 28-30 March 2006; Portland, OR. Proc. RMRS-P-41. Fort Collins, CO: U.S. Department of Agriculture, Forest Service, Rocky Mountain Research Station: 615-631.

Jain, Theresa B.; Pilliod, David S.; Graham, Russell T.; [and others]. 2012. Index for characterizing postfire soil environments in temperate coniferous forests. Forests. 13(3) 445-466.

Kasischke, E.S.; Turetsky, Merritt R.; Ottmar, Roger D.; [and others]. 2008. Evaluation of the composite burn index for assessing fire seerity in Alaskan black spruce forests. International Journal of Wildland Fire. 17: 515-526.

Keane, Robert E.; Reinhardt, Elizabeth; Brown, Jim; Gangi, Larry. 2008. First Order Fire Effects Model. V. 5.7. Missoula, MT: U.S. Department of Agriculture, Forest Service, Rocky Mountain Research Station, Fire Sciences Laboratory, http://www.firelab.org/science-applications/fire-fuel/111-fofem.

Keeley, Jon E. 2009. Fire intensity, fire severity and burn severity: A brief review and suggested usage. International Journal of Wildland Fire. 18: 116-126.

Key, C.H. 2005. Remote sensing sensitivity to fire severity and fire recovery. In: Proceedings of the 5th International Workshop on remote sensing and GIS applications to forest fire management: Fire effects assessment; June 16-18, 2005; Zarogoza, Spain: 29-39.

Key, C.H. 2006. Ecological and sampling constraints on defining landscape fire severity. Fire Ecology. 2(2): 178-203.

Key, C.H.; Benson, N.C. 1999. Measuring and remote sensing of burn severity: The CBI and NBR. Poster abstract. In: Neuenschwander, L.F.; Ryan, K.C., eds. Proceedings, Joint Fire Science Conference and Workshop, Vol. II; June 15-17, 1999; Boise, ID. University of Idaho and International Association of Wildland Fire. 284 p.

Key, C.H.; Benson, N.C. 2006. Landscape assessment: Ground measure of severity, the Composite Burn Index, and remote sensing of severity, the Normalized Burn Ratio. In: Lutes, D.C.; Keane, Robert E.; Caratti, J.F.; Key, C.H.; Benson, N.C.; Sutherland, S; Gangi, Larry. FIREMON: Fire effects monitoring and inventory system. Gen. Tech. Rep. RMRS-GTR-164-CD. Fort Collins, CO: U.S. Department of Agriculture, Forest Service, Rocky Mountain Research Station.

Kotliar, N.B.; Reynolds, E.W.; Deutschman, Douglas H. 2003. American three-toed woodpecker response to burn severity and prey. Fire Ecology Special Issue. 4(2): 26-45.

Kuenzi, Amanda M.; Fule, Peter Z.; Sieg, Carolyn Hull. 2008. Effects of fire severity and pre-fire stand treatment on plant community recovery after a large wildfire. Forest Ecology and Management. 255: 855-865.

Lentile, Leigh B.; Holden, Z.A.; Smith, A.M.; [and others]. 2006. Remote sensing techniques to assess active fire characteristics and post-fire effects. International Journal of Wildland Fire. 15: 319-345.

Lentile, Leigh B.; Morgan, Penelope; Hudak, Andrew T.; [and others]. 2007. Post-fire burn severity and vegetation response following eight large wildfires across the western United States. Fire Ecology. 3(1): 91-108.

Lewis, S.A.; Wu, J.Q.; Robichaud, P.R. 2006. Assessing burn severity and comparing soil water repellency, Hayman Fire, Colorado. Hydrological Processes. 20: 1-16.

Linn, Rodman; Winterkamp, Judith; Colman, Jonah J.; [and others]. 2005. Modeling interactions between fire and atmosphere in discrete element fuel beds. International Journal of Wildland Fire. 14: 37-48.

Lutes, Duncan C.; Keane, Robert E.; Caratti, John F. 2009. A surface fuel classification for estimating fire effects. International Journal of Wildland Fire. 18: 802-814.

Lutes, Duncan C.; Keane, Robert. E.; Caratti, John. F.; [and others]. 2006. FIREMON: Fire effects monitoring and inventory system. Gen. Tech. Rep. RMRS-GTR-164-CD. Fort Collins, CO: U.S. Department of Agriculture, Forest Service, Rocky Mountain Research Station. 1 CD.

McCune, B.; Grace, J.B. 2002. Analysis of ecological communities, Gleneden Beach, OR: MjM software Design. 300 p.

Miller, Jay D.; Nyhan, John W.; Yool, Stephen R. 2003. Modeling potential erosion due to the Cerro Grande Fire with a GIS-biased implementation of the Revised Universal Soil Loss Equation. International Journal of Wildland Fire. 12(1): 85-100.

Miller, Jay D.; Thode, Andrea E. 2007. Quantifying burn severity in a heterogeneous landscape with a relative version of the delta Normalized Burn Ratio (dNBR). Remote Sensing of Environment. 109(1): 66-80.

Moreno, Jose M.; Oechel, W.C. 1989. A simple method for estimating fire intensity after a burn in California chaparral. Acta Oecologica Oecologia Plantarum. 10: 57-68.

Morgan, Penelope; Hardy, Colin C.; Swetnam, Thomas W.; [and others]. 2001. Mapping fire regimes across time and space: Understanding coarse and fine-scale fire patterns. International Journal of Wildland Fire. 10: 329-342.

Murphy, Karen A.; Reynolds, Joel H.; Koltu, John M. 2008. Evaluating the ability of the differenced Normalized Burn Ratio (dNBR) to predict ecologically significant burn severity in Alaskan boreal forests. International Journal of Wildland Fire. 17: 490-499.

National Wildfire Coordinating Group (NWCG). 2006. Glossary of wildland fire terminology. U.S. Department of Agriculture, Forest Service; U.S. Department of the Interior, Bureau of Land Management, National Park Service, Bureau of Indian Affairs, Fish and Wildlife Service; National Wildfire Coordinating Group, Incident Operations Standards Working Team.

Nisbet, R.; Elder, J.; Miner, G. 2009. Handbook of statistical analysis and data mining applications. London: Elsevier. 824 p.

Norton, J.; Glenn, N.; Germino, M.; Weber, K.; Seefeldt, S. 2009. Relative suitability of indices derived from Landsat ETM+ and SPOT 5 for detecting fire severity in sagebrush stepp. International Journal of Applied Earth Observation and Geoinformation. 11: 360-367.

O'Brien, Kelly. 2004. Fuels planning: science synthesis and integration; forest structure and fire hazard fact sheet 2: Fire hazard. Res. Note RMRS-RN-22-2-WWW. Ogden, UT: U.S. Department of Agriculture, Forest Service, Rocky Mountain Research Station. 2 p.

Ottmar, Roger D.; Sandberg, David V.; Riccardi, C. L.; Prichard, S.J. 2007. An overview of the Fuel Characteristic Classification System—Quantifying, classifying, and creating fuelbeds for resource planning. Canadian Journal Forest Research. 37(12): 2383-2393.

Parsons, A. 2003. Burned Area Emergency Rehabilitation (BAER) soil burn severity definitions and mapping guidelines. Draft. U.S. Department of Agriculture, Forest Service. 12 p. Online: http://www.fws.gov/fire/ifcc/esr/Remote%20Sensing/soil_burnsev_summary_guide042203.pdf. [May 10, 2012].

Parsons, Annette; Robichaud, Peter R.; Lewis, Sarah A.; [and others]. 2010. Field guide for mapping post-fire soil burn severity. Gen. Tech. Rep. RMRS-GTR-243. Fort Collins, CO: U.S. Department of Agriculture, Forest Service, Rocky Mountain Research Station. 49 p.

Parsons, Russell; Mell, William E.; McCauley, Peter. 2011. Linking 3D spatial models of fuels and fire: Effects of spatial heterogeneity on fire behavior. Ecological Modelling. 222(3): 679-691.

Perez, Beatriz; Moreno, Jose M. 1998. Methods for quantifying fire severity in shrubland fires. Plant Ecology. 139: 91-101.

Prichard, S.J.; Ottmar, R.D.; Anderson, G.K. 2006. Consume 3.0 User's Guide. Seattle, WA: U.S. Department of Agriculture, Forest Service, Pacific Northwest Research Station, Pacific Wildland Fire Sciences Laboratory, Fire and Environmental Research Applications Team. 234 p.

Redmond, Roland L.; Winne, Chris. 2001. Classifying and mapping wildfire severity. Imaging Notes. Sept/Oct: 3 p.

Reinhardt, Elizabeth; Keane, Robert E. 1998. FOFEM—A First Order Fire Effects Model. Fire Management Notes. 58(2): 25-28.

Reinhardt, Elizabeth; Keane, Robert E.; Brown, James K. 1997. First Order Fire Effects Model: FOFEM 4.0 User's Guide. Gen. Tech. Rep. INT-344. Ogden, UT: U.S. Department of Agriculture, Forest Service, Intermountain Research Station. 65 p.

Robichaud, P.R.; Elliot, W.J.; Pierson, F.B.; [and others]. 2007a. Predicting postfire erosion and mitigation effectiveness with a web-based probabilistic erosion model. CATENA. 72(2): 229-241.

Robichaud, P.R.; Lewis, S.A.; Laes, Denise Y.M.; [and others]. 2007b. Postfire soil burn severity mapping with hyperspectral image unmixing. Remote Sensing of Environment. 108: 467-480.

Robichaud, P.R.; MacDonald, Lee; Freeouf, Jeff; [and others]. 2003. Postfire rehabilitation of the Hayman Fire. In: Graham, Russell T. Hayman Fire Case Study. Gen. Tech. Rep. RMRS-GTR-114. Ogden, UT: U.S. Department of Agriculture, Forest Service, Rocky Mountain Research Station: 293-313.

Rothermel, R. C. 1972. A mathematical model for predicting fire spread in wildland fuels. Res. Pap. INT-115. Ogden, UT: U.S. Department of Agriculture, Forest Service, Intermountain Forest and Range Experiment Station. 40 p.

Ryan, K.C.; Noste, N.V. 1985. Evaluating prescribed fires. In: Lotan, J.E.; Kilgore, B.M.; Fischer, W.C.; Mutch, R.W., eds. Proceedings, symposium and workshop on wilderness fire; 15-18 November 1983; Missoula, MT: Gen. Tech. INT-182. Ogden, UT: U.S. Department of Agriculture, Forest Service, Intermountain Forest and Range Experiment Station: 230-238.

Ryan, Kevin C. 2002. Dynamic interactions between forest structure and fire behavior in boreal ecosystems. Silva Fennica. 36(1): 13-39.

SAS Institute Inc. 2008. SAS for Windows, Cary, NC.

Schimmel, Johnny; Granstrom, Anders. 1996. Fire severity and vegetation response in the boreal Swedish forest. Ecology. 77(5): 1436-1450.

Simard, A.J. 1991. Fire severity, changing scales, and how things hang together. International Journal of Wildland Fire. 1(1): 23-34.

Singh, A. 1989. Digital change detection techniqes using remotely-sensed data. International Journal of Remote Sensing. 10(6): 989-1003.

Systat Software Inc. 2008. SigmaPlot for Windows San Jose, CA.

Tarrant, R.F. 1956. Effect of slashburning on some physical soil properties. Forest Science. 2: 19-22.

Trowbridge, R.; Schmidt, S.; Bedford, L. 1989. Slashburning severity guidelines for the moist cold sub-boreal spruce subzone (SBSmc) in the Prince Rupert forest region British Columbia. Victoria, BC: British Columbia Ministry of Forestry.

Turner, Monica G.; Romme, William H.; Gardner, Robert H. 1999. Prefire heterogenity, fire severity, and early postfire plant reestablishment in subalpine forests of Yellowstone National Park, Wyoming. International Journal of Wildland Fire. 9(1): 21-36.

Turner, Monica G.; William W. Hargrove; Robert H. Gardner; Romme, William H. 1994. Effects of fire on landscape heterogeneity in Yellowstone National Park, Wyoming. Journal of Vegetation Science. 5: 731-742.

U.S. Department of Agriculture. 2010. Wildfire burn severity classification. Bozeman, MT: U.S. Department of Agriculture, Natural Resources Conservation Service, Montana State Office. Online: http://www mt nrcs.usda.gov/technical/eng/ewp/severity html. [May 10, 2012].

U.S. Department of the Interior. 2011. LANDFIRE: LANDFIRE 1.1.0 Fuel Layer Product Descriptions. U.S. Department of the Interior, U.S. Geological Survey. [http://landfire. cr.usgs.gov/viewer/, last accessed 5/14/2012].

van Wagendonk, Jan W.; Root, Ralph R.; Key, Carl H. 2004. Comparison of AVIRIS and Landsat ETM+ detection capabilities for burn severity. Remote Sensing of Environment. 92(3): 397-408.

Venables, W.N.; Ripley, B.D. 2002. Modern Applied Statistics with S—PLUS. New York: Springer-Verlag.

Wang, Cheng; Glenn, Nancy F. 2009. Estimation of fire severity using pre- and post-fire LiDAR data in sagebrush steppe rangelands. International Journal of Wildland Fire. 18: 848-856.

Wells, C.G.; DeBano, L.F.; Lewis, C.E.; [and others]. 1979. Effects of fire on soil: A state-of-knowledge review. Gen. Tech. Rep. WO-7. Washington, DC: U.S. Department of Agricultue, Forest Service. 34 p.

White, Joseph D.; Ryan, Kevin C.; Key, Carl C.; Running, Steven W. 1996. Remote sensing of forest fire severity and vegetation recovery. International Journal of Wildland Fire. 6(3): 125-136.

Zarriello, T.J.; Knick, S.T.; Rotenberry, J.T. 1995. Producing a burn/disturbance map for the Snake River Birds of Prey National Conservation Area. Boise, ID: U.S. Department of the Interior, Bureau of Land Management.

Appendix A—Ranges of fuel components and moisture characteristics for each class in the synthetic data set (N = 115,280).

Range of duff biomass within each of nine classes. Classes created by agglomerative clustering of 115,280 fuel beds and five variables. Box and whisker plots show the 25th percentile (lower edge of box), median (line within box), the 75th percentile (upper edge of box, extreme upper and lower values [whiskers from box], and outliers (circles).

A. Range of duff within each of the nine classes.

B. Range of litter within each of the nine classes.

C. Range of 1-hr fuels within each of the nine classes.

D. Range of 10-hr fuels within each of the nine classes.

E. Range of 100-hr fuels within each of the nine classes.

F. Range of coarse woody debris values within each of the nine classes.

G. Range of duff moisture values within each of the nine classes for duff layers comprising each fuel bed.

H. Range of moisture values within each of nine classes for the 10-hr fuels component of each fuel bed.

I. Range of moisture values within each of nine classes for the coarse woody debris fuels component of each fuel bed.

J. Range of moisture values within each of the nine classes for the soil moisture component of each fuel bed.

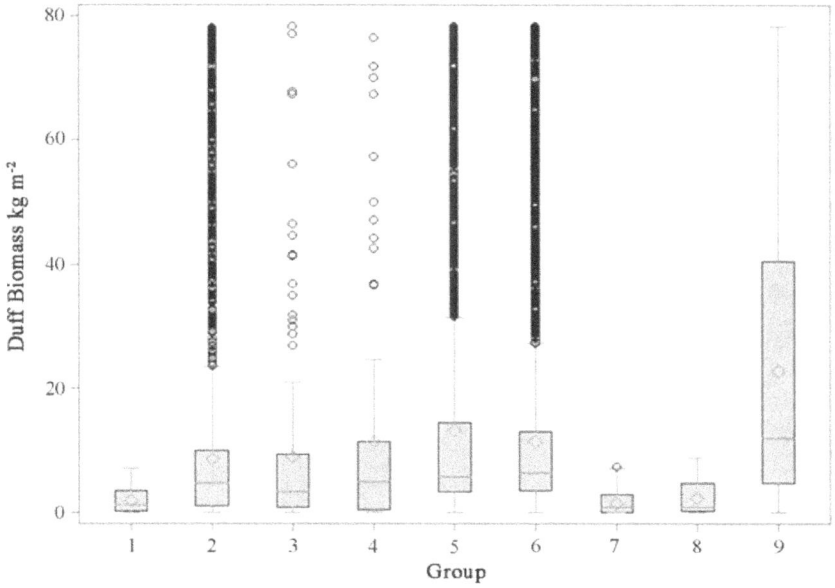

A. Range of duff within each of the nine classes.

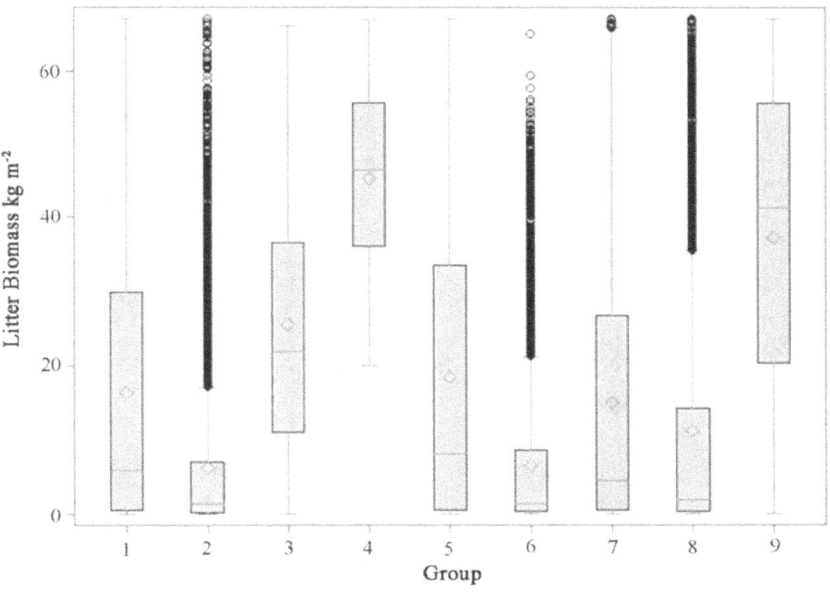

B. Range of litter fuels within each of the nine classes.

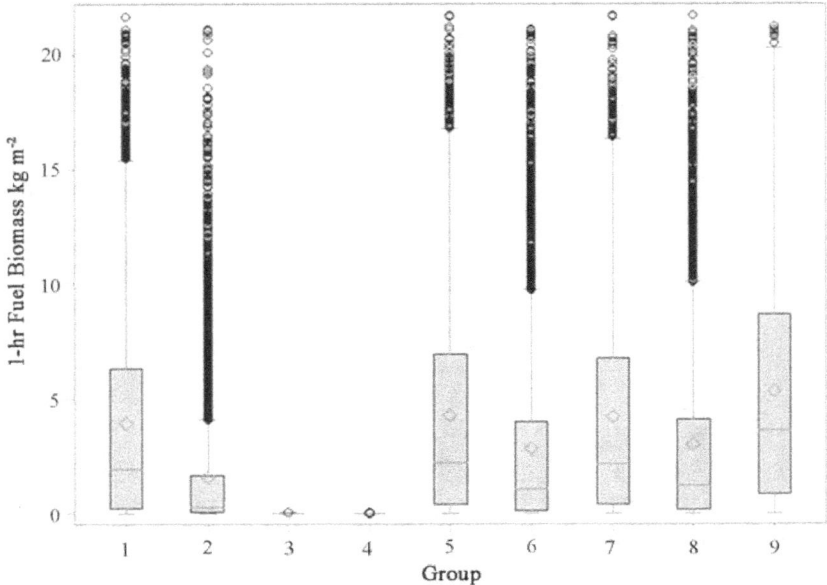

C. Range of 1-hr fuels within each of the nine classes.

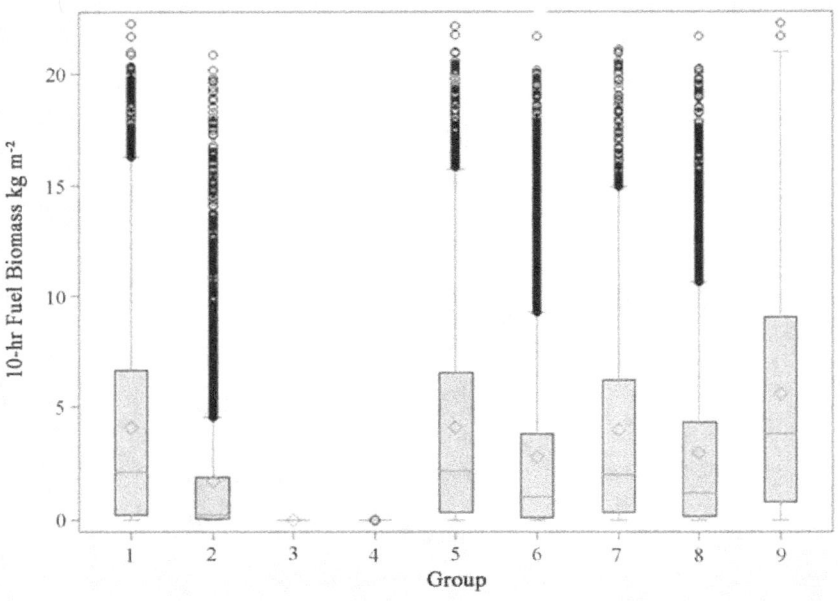

D. Range of 10-hr fuels within each of the nine classes.

USDA Forest Service RMRS-RP-96. 2012.

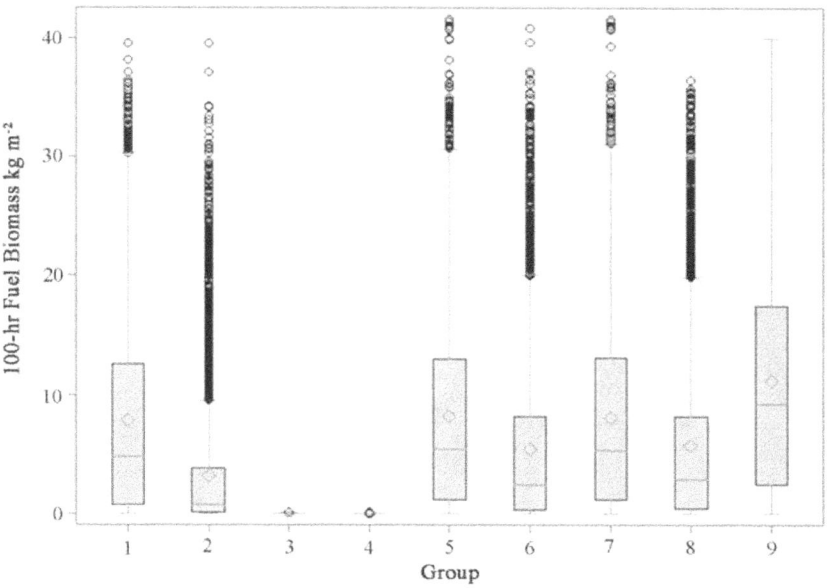

E. Range of 100-hr fuels values within each of the nine classes.

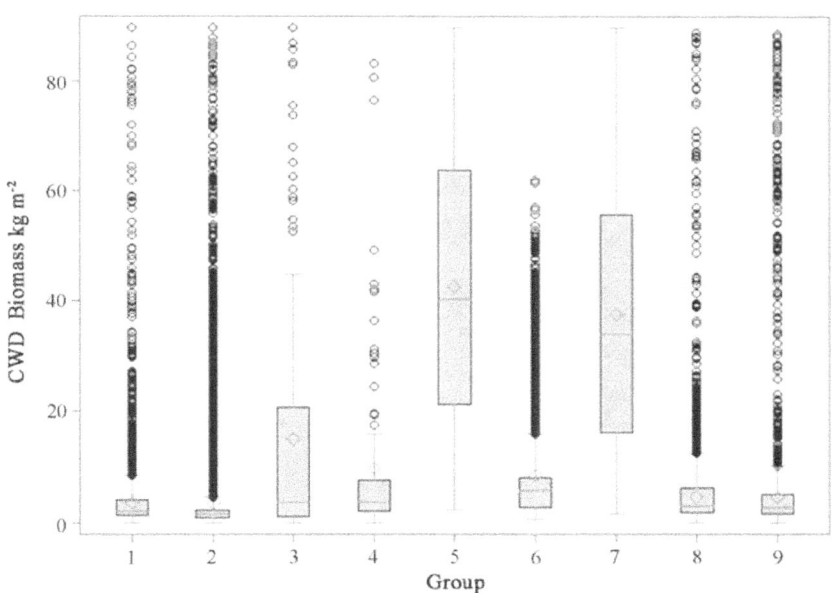

F. Range of coarse woody debris within each of the nine classes for duff layers comprising each fuel bed.

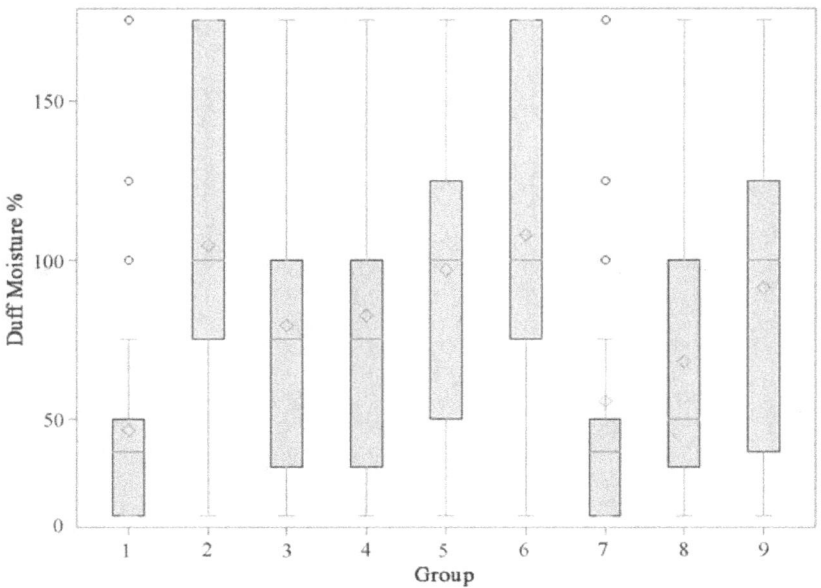

G. Range of duff moisture values within each of the nine classes for duff layers comprising each fuel bed.

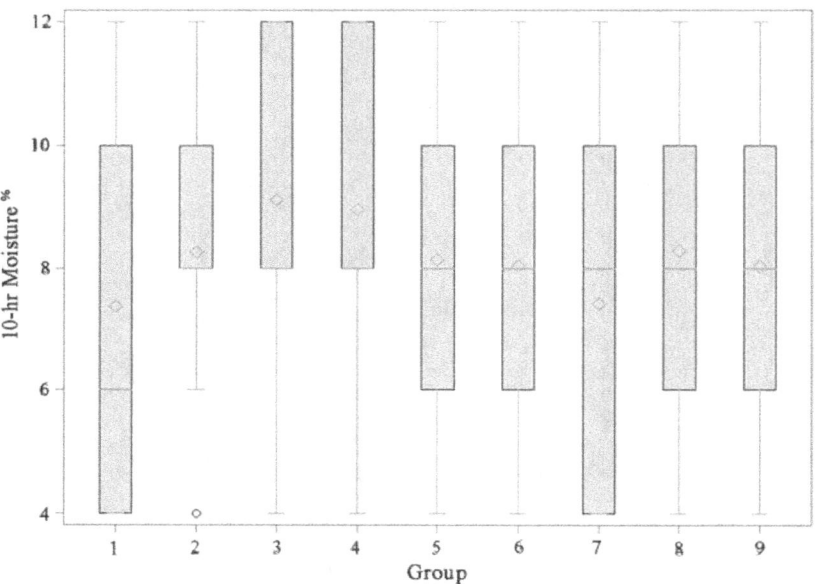

H. Range of moisture values within each of nine classes for the 10-hr fuels component of each fuel bed.

USDA Forest Service RMRS-RP-96. 2012.

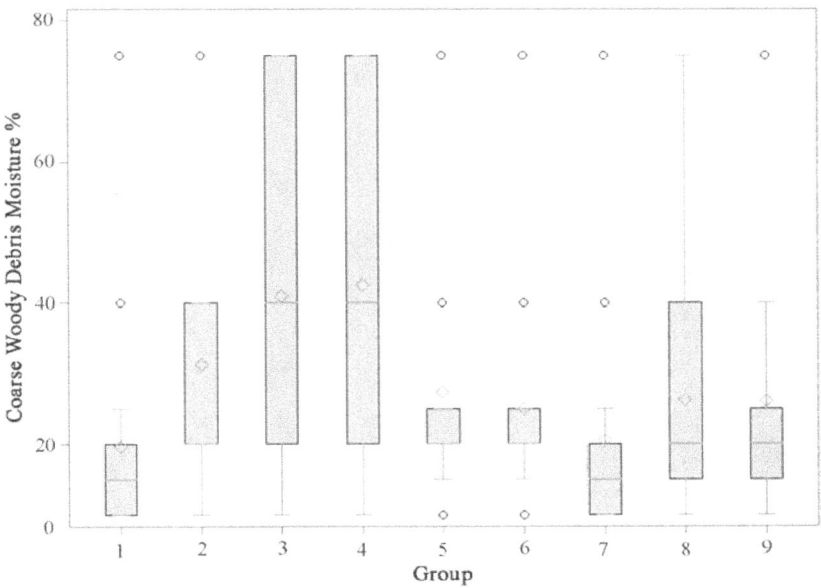

I. Range of moisture values within each of nine classes for the coarse woody debris fuels component of each fuel bed.

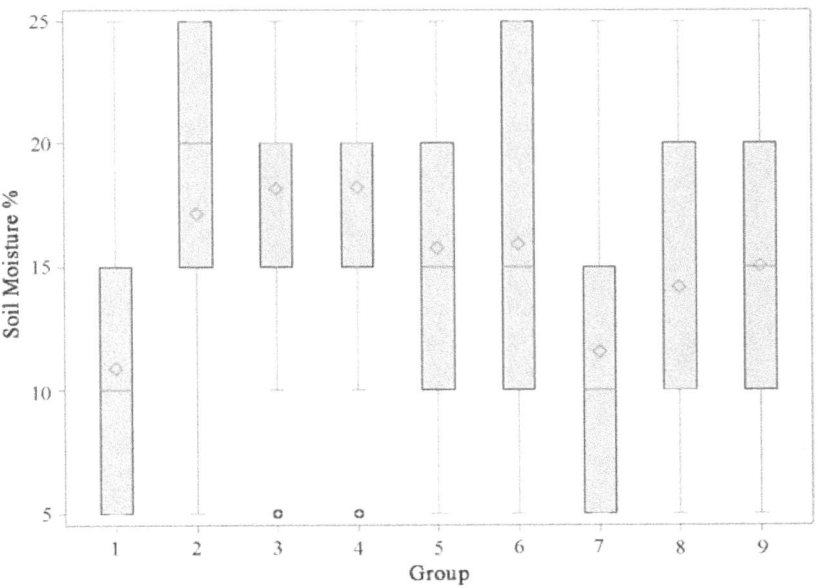

J. Range of moisture values within each of the nine classes for the soil moisture component of each fuel bed.